# Emerg

*Today, in this crucial moment of history, we are called to recover the inner vision of a society in harmony with nature, and the urgency of reciprocity of care between ourselves and our environment.*

*This newly recognized relationship between us and the surrounding natural world rests on our experience of its wonder, beauty, and call to intimacy. In preserving and augmenting these responses, we realize, perhaps never before so vividly, that, as the consciousness of that world, we have an indispensable role to play. More than just protection against pollution and extinction of life forms, that role calls us, further, to revere Earth as that community of which we are a part, the source of our life and livelihood, and, above all, the primary means of our recognition of and communication with the divine.*

*The Center for Education, Imagination and the Natural World is dedicated to the recovery of the inner vision of a society in harmony with nature. The Center restores a relationship with the natural world based, not on a view of other beings as objects to be used, but as subjects to be communed with in an integral and sacred society.*

*The Center is a perfect context for the continuity of this work with children and the sacred. It has brought joy in the last years of my life, for the children have always been closest to my heart.*

~ Thomas Berry, July 2008

Since the Center's beginnings in 2000, educators, naturalists, therapists, parents and others with children in their care have gathered in listening circles to consider how we might recover the inner vision of a society in harmony with nature and explore in co-presence our unique roles and voices in creating a reciprocity of care between human beings and the natural world. In 2011, the Center published *Only the Sacred: Transforming Education in the*

*Twenty-first Century*, a collection of essays by 27 educators who have been part of this process.

Now, in 2015, we offer our Emergence Series of publications authored by those close to the Center who have carried the work forward in new and promising ways in written form. In the spirit of a communion of subjects, they have gifted their books to the Center. All proceeds from book sales will return to the Center in support of its work.

# I Am You, You Are Me

*The Interrelatedness of*
*Self, Spirituality and the Natural World in Childhood*

## Colette Segalla

The Center for Education, Imagination and the Natural World
2015

ISBN: 978-0-692-52906-5

The article "Rare Photo Found of Slave Children" is reprinted
with permission of the Associated Press.

Published by
The Center for Education, Imagination
and the Natural World
P.O. Box 41108
Greensboro, NC
www.beholdnature.org

## Dedication

For John.

You were not forgotten.

I remember you.

# CONTENTS

# Acknowledgements

I would like to acknowledge Dr. Robert Romanyshyn, Dr. Jennifer Selig, and Dr. Tobin Hart, for being my guides and supporters throughout the research process. Each of them has been an inspiration to me.

I would also like to acknowledge the many friends and family members who tolerated my necessary, single-minded focus on my work throughout the research process.

I had the very good fortune to have been offered a writing sanctuary in the beautiful home of friends, Beth Briggs and Hank Wall, when I simply had to work outside my own home. This gave me the space and peace I needed to make the final push to complete this study.

Gina Roberts offered true friendship and wisdom to me at key points during the research process. She also helped me see the path through the forest in order to complete the study.

Carolyn Toben and Peggy Whalen-Levitt have been spiritual guides and way-showers for me, beginning with my first introduction to The Center for Education, Imagination and the Natural World. The amazing work of these two women, their friendship, and their wisdom has been a critical part of this work. They have been key figures in the synthesis and culmination of everything that went into this study.

I wish to acknowledge my spiritual guide and supporter through all of the ups and downs of this transformational journey, Rachael Wooten. Without her wise presence and accompaniment, it is highly doubtful I would have made it to the other side.

I gratefully acknowledge both of my parents for their love, their love of the natural world, and for providing the foundation for my spiritual sense of self. I have often said that I must have good karma to have been born to my parents, along with my two brothers and two sisters. I especially appreciate guidance and encouragement from my mother, Rosemary, and brother, Roger, as colleagues in the field of psychology. They patiently read drafts of the study and offered much helpful feedback. They also provided a much needed call from the other side of darkness, helping me find my way through.

I am also grateful and would like to acknowledge my three stepdaughters, Cameo, Amy, and Mandy for the co-creation of our blended family. What a gift to be mother to three such lovely women who have taught me so much. They, too, have been an important part of this journey.

Finally, I certainly would not have been able to complete the book, if I had not had the unending support of my best friend and husband, Tom Edwards. This accomplishment belongs to both of us.

# Introduction

When I was a child, during a moment of quiet contemplation, I asked myself, "What if I did not exist?" Rather than just quickly dismissing the question as unanswerable, I grappled with this question. "Really, what if I just did not exist?" Suddenly my imagination took me outside of myself, to space, where the mystery of life manifested for me as sacred darkness ever so slightly illuminated by the white light of tiny stars. I can relive that experience easily and recall how my question was answered from within this imagery: I would have no way of knowing what it would be like not to exist, because if I did not exist I could not ask the question of what it would be like to not exist; therefore, it would be useless to compare the state of nonexistence to my current state in order to determine which would be better. Whereas nonexistence seemed impossible to me, I reasoned,

> If I did not exist as me, then I would have to exist as someone else. Otherwise, I would not be able to ask this question. So if I did not exist as me, and I would therefore exist as someone else, what is the difference between existing as me and existing as someone else?

I pondered this question in silence, with the same image of the starry night sky filling my imagination. I eventually concluded, "Nothing. There would be no difference between existing as me or existing as someone else, because whoever I was existing as, I would identify as 'me.' I would still have the experience of existing as an individual self, unable to know what it would truly mean to not exist." Based on this contemplation, a short poem formed in my mind:

I am you
You are me
We are all
All are we.

We cannot judge one another
for if we do,
It would be as though

I were not you
You were not me
We were not all
All were not we.

I wrote this poem in a small notepad with the drawing of a dog on the cover. The "revelations" then continued. In this "space" of what I would now call "cosmic consciousness," I had the sense that I must have *chosen* to be born. "If I chose this—to be alive—then, although I feel miserable, if I can make sense of it and learn from it, it must be meaningful, rather than just miserable. There must be something I am here to learn." My ponderings continued: "If I chose to be here, and this life is all about learning and growing, then this must be a place where souls come to learn and grow. Earth is like a school, then." I began to think more personally about myself as a soul who had chosen to come here to learn and grow. The thought came to me that I had probably lived many times before and had learned much but still had much to learn. For me, the purpose of living became centered on spiritual growth.

Before the day I contemplated what it would be like for me not to exist, I had not received much indoctrination on matters of the spirit. My family did go to church on holidays up until I was about 8 years old; instead, we had a special Christmas ritual we practiced when I was very young that involved a procession and the placing of the baby Jesus in the manger late on Christmas Eve. As far as being told who or what God was, or what was the nature of my own spirit, or anything that would have oriented me to a spiritual perspective through doctrine and dogma, however, I did not have a storehouse of ideas informing my conscious perspective. In later years, I began to feel grateful that I had not been indoctrinated into any formalized religion, because I felt that having my own spiritual experiences or revelations was more meaningful to me than being told or taught about God and the nature of life.

Questioning my existence and writing the poem, which took place when I was 10 or 11 years old, was a foundational spiritual experience of transcendence and making meaning in my life. It became for me a guidepost to which I returned time and again in order to maintain my orientation as to the purpose of my life. I thought of myself in a life-long growth process, and thus, subsequent times of challenge, opportunity, or misery led me to ask repeatedly, "What am I to learn from this? How do I integrate this experience with my spiritual perspective on life?"

When I made choices about college, career, and family, I returned to this guidepost and tried to determine whether a given option resonated with what felt like the deepest part of myself—that part where my ultimate purpose for living resided and which I knew to be my essential self. Once I had the experience of cosmic consciousness just described, my life choices would be evaluated from that perspective. I became more acutely attuned to my inner world through the experience of transcendence, and this deep awareness seemed to permeate my sense of self in the world.

I would not always remember the words of the poem or be able to live from the truth of them, but my way of being in the world was still greatly affected by the experience and its impact on my sense of self and perspective on life. Was it the only experience to have an impact on my sense of self? Certainly not. Was it the only "spiritual" experience that I had as a child? Again, with certainty, no. Many other instances occurred; however, this experience was a discreet, memorable, and a defining event that had a lasting effect.

As an adult, I took this experience and its impact on me for granted. The memory of the poem and the accompanying insight receded in my consciousness, but from time to time, it would resurface on a conscious level. One of those times was when I began to revisit what was, by then, a dormant idea to study psychology. By that time, I had been teaching in a Montessori school for many years.

The children I taught in the Montessori school were ages 6 to 9 years old. When I first set out upon my teaching career, however, I had never actually intended to teach such young children. Originally, I was certified to teach secondary school and taught 3 years of eighth grade Language Arts. While teaching the eighth grade in a public school, I soon began to recognize that the school system was lacking in a cohesive philosophy and was wrought with overwhelming dysfunction. At that time, upon hearing my concerns, some friends offered to introduce me to someone who worked at the Montessori school their children attended. The school was expanding into the middle school grades and this person was developing a middle school curriculum. After meeting this person and learning about the Montessori philosophy, I considered transitioning to Montessori education, which would involve returning to school for Montessori teacher training. My hope was that once I obtained the necessary teacher certification, I could apply for a middle school position at that school, which by the then would be hiring additional teachers.

At that point, however, I chose not to pursue Montessori teacher training, because it would involve a relocation and the disruption of a relationship with the person who was to become my husband. Several weeks later, however, I received a phone call from one of the administrators at the Montessori school. She asked me to consider working with younger children. When I reminded her that I was not Montessori certified, she told me that the school would sponsor me in the training. Although this was unexpected, the Montessori philosophy and methodology resonated so strongly with me that I decided to accept the offer. My mindset had already been shaped by the idea that my life was about spiritual growth. I had found that the most valuable experiences came about when I was open to unexpected opportunities that intuitively seemed to be a positive step on a path of growth. This was my established way of proceeding through my life and decision-making, rather than with a linear pursuit of intellectually conceived career ambitions. Although completing the training would involve traveling from North Carolina to California for three summers and teaching during the school year, I felt that "Life" had guided me to this point, and I was grateful for the guidance. In my mind, this was part of my path of growth.

The Montessori teacher training proved to be a rich and rewarding experience. While in the training program, one of the aspects that resonated most profoundly with me was the foundational idea that each child is born with a unique potential to be discovered and fulfilled throughout his or her lifetime. The educational method was designed to help facilitate the natural unfolding and realization of this potential. In the classroom, I found an enormous difference in working with children from this standpoint rather than from the standpoint of trying to ensure that all students passed their state mandated end-of-grade tests. In addition, being immersed in the Montessori philosophy and methodology further stimulated my interest in spirituality and, more particularly, as it concerns children.

I counted myself lucky to have been befriended and guided by a long time Montessorian in this transition from working with older children in a public school setting to working with younger children in a Montessori environment. Although teaching children in any setting requires compassion and empathy for the child, the work in the Montessori classroom of 6 to 9-year-olds required more emphasis on empathizing with the child, or coming from a heart-centered place than from an intellectual place, as was the case with the students in the eighth grade where I had previously taught. In the process of making the shift from the safety of the intellect to the complexity of the heart, I began sifting through my own childhood experiences. This form of self-reflection in a context of young children was new to me and put me in touch with the formative nature and significance of these middle childhood years. I knew even then that at some point in the future I wanted to transition to the field of psychology and this seemed an important part of the "know thyself" proposition with which prospective therapists enter the field. To me, it made sense that I would benefit from this experience as part of a preparation for taking my next step.

After many years in the classroom, I began to consider my next step toward entering the field of psychology. I knew that I would need to find a program that integrated the spiritual dimension of being human into the study of psychology, because my orientation to life had been so clearly shaped by what seemed to me to be the reciprocal interaction between my inner spiritual life, my own personal choices, and the opportunities and circumstances of my life. I did not feel the pull to enter the field when I looked into programs that did not have a depth orientation with potential of inclusion of the spiritual. Eventually, I found a program that suited me, at Pacifica Graduate Institute, once again in California, and once again not the most rational of options, for it would involve monthly treks to California from North Carolina. Nonetheless, I decided to follow this course of action based, once again, on the strong resonance I felt with the program and because it "fit" with my perspective that my pursuits should facilitate and encourage spiritual growth.

Just as I was about to begin the program at Pacifica, I received a phone call from an acquaintance I had recently met through a mutual friend. Over the phone, this acquaintance, who was soon to become a very dear friend, was relieved to have reached me after having lost the contact information I had given her when we met. She went on to explain that her organization, The Center for Education, Imagination and the Natural World (CEINW), had recently been awarded a grant. CEINW would be conducting a 2-year program for educators, The Inner Life of the Child in Nature (ILCN), and as I was a Montessori teacher, she wanted me to apply for a place in it. Although I explained to her that I was just about to begin my graduate studies, she assured me that I would be able to participate in her program simultaneously.

The ILCN program fit extremely well with my interest in children's spirituality, which I had hoped to explore more deeply in graduate school. ILCN is a program that was designed to work with adults in the natural world in such a way that they actually experience the deep and spiritual connection possible with nature in order that they, in turn, can facilitate connection between the children they work with and the natural world. The ultimate mission of the Center is to work toward raising consciousness by redefining and re-visioning the human relationship with nature.

After I began my graduate coursework at Pacifica, I found that the work with CEINW was like a hinge connecting my work as a Montessori teacher of young children with my studies in Jungian-oriented depth psychology. Although I set out with an interest in the spiritual life of the child, I was amazed to see how things unfolded in such a way to support this interest in what seemed like such a personalized fashion. In the case of both transitions, first into the field of

Montessori education and then into the field of depth psychology, I had received what seemed like timely guidance from within the fields to which I was transitioning.

Musings about these transitions and about the continuity of experiences that contributed to my sense of self have further stimulated my curiosity about children's spirituality. How did my spiritual orientation become the organizing principle around which I developed a sense of self? How did this element of my way of conceptualizing myself in my life become an inherent aspect of my being? What sense can I make of the synchronicity of beginning my work at Pacifica with an interest in children's spirituality and being asked to participate in the educator's program at CEINW? Where does an experienced relationship with the natural world fit in with the picture of a child's spirituality and spiritual growth? I also began to wonder about the role of my connection with nature in the development of a spiritual sense of self. Why does the natural world always seem to have guided me in my spiritual development? How has it guided me through internal images and metaphoric thinking? These personal mysteries led me to my research question: How does spirituality influence a child's development of a sense of self and how is this mediated by a relationship with nature? What are the relationships between sense of self, spirituality and the natural world?

In pursuing my interest in these questions beginning with a preliminary research paper in 2007, I found that the question of spirituality in children had not been widely discussed in the field of clinical psychology, especially when the question of a relationship with the natural world is part of the research. As shown in the literature review, inquiry into the significance of the child's relationship with the natural world exists, but what appears to be lacking is research on how this experienced relationship and its potentially spiritual quality contribute to the psychospiritual development of the child.

The autobiographical origins of my interest in this topic clearly indicate that many personal influences would make their way into this research process. I assume, for one, that human life has a purpose; I do not see it as purposeless before the point when we create meaning of our experiences. More specifically, I believe that the primary and most fundamental purpose of human life is spiritual growth. Another predisposition to this topic is that the spiritual nature of human beings cannot, in reality, be separated from a psychological understanding of human beings; furthermore, the psychological description of a human being must be embedded within a spiritual context, rather than the reverse. I am also firmly biased toward the notion that human beings are essentially good and striving toward a higher good. Coming from a Western culture, which is oriented toward the individual (as opposed to the communal), I assume that spiritual growth can and does take place on an individual basis. My hidden agenda may be to promote the notion that spiritual growth is the ultimate purpose of human life. In addition, this pursuit is fueled by the hope that in recognizing the significance of spiritual growth to the life-purpose of human beings, this process of spiritual growth will be better supported and promoted in therapeutic and educational settings as well as in society at large. My hope is also that spiritual growth as a fundamental purpose of human life may be acknowledged no matter the culture or religion in which a person lives.

This perspective helped to narrow the scope of the current study in that I will not attempt to answer the question of the ultimate purpose of spirituality and spiritual development. With this limit already in place, the study could focus more precisely on how the development of a sense of self is affected by one's spiritual nature and the process of spiritual development. Without limiting the scope of this inquiry, the study would be bound to attempt to define the aim of spiritual development, because the term *development* implies a progression and a progression implies an ultimate goal or aim. In actuality, the phrase *spiritual development* carries an implicit acknowledgement of some goal or aim, although in most of the literature, as indicated in the following review, the *ultimate* goal or aim is not clearly stated. Clearly, no empirical way exists to prove or disprove the purpose of life as I have stated it; thus, I have claimed it as a predisposition.

At this time, to my knowledge, there is currently no literature or research in clinical psychology offering a depth psychological understanding of the ways in which spirituality, sense of self, and the natural world are interrelated in children. Considering the current cultural climate in the industrialized world of controversy and conflict over global environmental concerns, combined with a lack of understanding of the psychological impact of these environmental issues on the healthy development of children, as well as a lack of understanding on how both spirituality and a relationship with the natural world contribute to the development of a sense of self, research that attempts to further the understanding of the interrelatedness between spirituality, self, and the natural world seems timely if not overdue. Through environmental movements and other vehicles of widespread communication (such as Al Gore's film, *An Inconvenient Truth*), the prospect of global environmental devastation and the end of life as we know it has increasingly becoming a part of collective understanding, as the growth of these movements and the inclusion of environmental topics in many local, state, and federal elections in the United States indicates. The prospect of environmental devastation, and in fact, the evidence of it in changing weather patterns, severe storms, flooding, drought, increased sea level, and massive extinctions seems to bring more sharply into focus existential considerations for what it means to be human on planet Earth. By itself, the scientific approach to resolving these issues strictly on the level of the environment is clearly not adequate, as the controversy and discord around environmental concerns demonstrates even while devastation from environmental catastrophes escalates.

An additional facet to the cultural climate that also calls for more research on this topic is the greater and increasing prevalence of indoor, electronics-based entertainment for children, taking the place of free play outdoors. Clearly, contemporary culture in the United States is moving in the direction of more electronics-based interaction in many aspects of everyday life. Without a clinical understanding of the contribution of both spirituality and a relationship with the natural world to the healthy development of children, how are we to determine whether this shift is healthy for children and whether this shift helps or hinders resolution of the undeniably significant environmental issues we currently face. Further, the spiritual life of the child, when not recognized, understood, or valued, is at risk of being neglected or inadvertently abused in the name of "progress," just as our environmental crises—from global warming to rainforest devastation to massive oil spills in our oceans, have all come about as a consequence and in the name of economic growth and "progress." Reexamination of our relationship with the earth might be considered, in itself, a spiritual pursuit, and one that may have a profound effect on the sense of self as well as on the natural world. Given these considerations, it seems to me that the need for research on the topic of the interrelatedness of self, spirituality, and the natural world in children is blatantly clear.

The following study is an exploration of the ways in which spirituality contributes to the development of a sense of self in children. Further, this study seeks to understand how the natural world plays a part in the interaction between self and spirituality. The study was conducted using an imaginal approach, with its processes and method of making a place for the unconscious, resulting in a theoretical depiction of the interpermeating (W. Adams, 1999) relationships between children's spirituality, sense of self, and the natural world.

*Chapter One*

# Toward A Deeper Understanding: The Hermeneutic Approach

In order to address this research question, I conducted a theoretical study using a hermeneutic method and its variation, alchemical hermeneutics. Hermeneutics is a research method that calls into question the positivist paradigm of objectivity (Camic, Rhodes, & Yardley, 2003). It is a method that acknowledges the ongoing creation of meaning in the field between a text and a reader of a text. The image for that interconnection is the hermeneutic circle. For the current study, therefore, rather than seeking an "objective" conception of reality, as if reality were fixed and static or an object of study, I sought a different kind of outcome – one that comes from a dialectical hermeneutic (Palmer, 1969) resulting in "not so much…understanding more correctly…as understanding more deeply, more truly" (p. 215).

More specifically, I used a qualitative, dialogic method comparing literature from three different areas. These three areas are children's spirituality, sense of self development, and the human–nature connection. A dialogue amongst these three areas was undertaken in order to elucidate the relationship and dynamics between self, spirituality, and the natural world. I am primarily interested in this relationship with regard to children and childhood; connections are drawn, however, between this relationship in childhood and the same relationship in later stages of life. This was done in the service of painting a more richly detailed theoretical picture of self and spirituality in childhood.

Although the critical conversation between these three bodies of literature focuses on the relationship in children between self, spirituality, and the natural world, by necessity the conversation involved a process of conceptual sifting and sorting to clarify and more precisely define the object of focus. The conceptual sifting and sorting involved placing literature from different disciplines or subdisciplines side by side within any one main body of literature. In other words, what are developmental psychologists saying, for example, about self and sense of self development versus what self psychologists and Jungian analytical psychologists are saying? Thus the study involves a nested set of text-based, dialogic engagements. On the first level, the dialogue occurs between researchers and theorists within each main realm of literature, followed by findings from these dialogues being placed in dialogic interaction with one another. Put another way, a triangular, three-way Venn diagram depicts an overlapping area shared by all three bodies of literature that is the central focus of the study. The point of the study was to find out exactly what the overlapping area between the three areas of literature entails, and subsequently, what results from this overlap. Was there a way to integrate the findings from this comparison such that something new reveals itself?

## The Text-Based Hermeneutic Method

The nature of my research question lends itself to a hermeneutic method of engaging and comparing literature from the three main areas of the question. The word *hermeneutics* has its etymological heritage in ancient Greek mythology and the messenger god, Hermes (Palmer, 1969). According to Graves's (1960) retelling of the myth of Hermes's childhood, Hermes earned the admonishment and praise of his father, Zeus, through acts of theft, trickery, and innovation as a child. Upon hearing from Apollo of Hermes's misdeeds, Zeus was impressed with his son and praised him for his cleverness but also warned against telling "downright lies" (p. 65). Hermes responded with a request to be his father's herald and the promise that he would "never tell lies, but" he continued, "I cannot promise always to tell the whole truth" (p. 65).

Hermeneutics acknowledges at the outset the philosophical trouble of the subject/object split found in scientific research (Palmer, 1969). In his introduction to the well known text, *Hermeneutics* (1969), Palmer quotes French phenomenologist Merleau-Ponty: "Science manipulates things and gives up living in them" (p. 7). In an attempt to sanitize the work, to cleanse it of any subjective contamination by the researcher, the positivistic, scientific approach ends up reporting on findings obtained from a dead object; the object of study has been killed and dissected in an effort to understand it. The insistence of "objectivity" in positivistic psychological research results in an unnatural separation between the researcher and that which is being researched. The separation is unnatural in that it assumes there is a way to get around the researcher to a clear space where the subjectivity of the researcher does not come into play. When it comes to understanding texts, rather than killing and dissecting, hermeneutics engages and interprets the text, which means the researcher, and his or her subjectivity, is necessarily part of the process. Palmer concisely summarizes: "Dialogue, not dissection, opens up a literary work" (p. 7).

**The hermeneutic circle.** Thus in hermeneutics, we find Hermes's promise holds true: in the process of interpretation, one never comes to the "whole truth" but engages instead in an ongoing process of making meaning with the text through dialogue and understanding (Palmer, 1969). Understanding involves a movement back and forth between what one knows to begin with and what one does not already know, a "dialectical interaction between the whole and the part, each [giving] the other meaning" (p. 87). This process is known as the hermeneutic circle.

**Hermeneutics as interpretation.** Each rotation within the hermeneutic circle involves interpretation; however, the meaning of interpretation itself is central to hermeneutics and also has particular relevance to this study. Palmer (1969) discusses the necessity of a "humanistic understanding of what interpretation of a work involves" (p. 7). He goes on to discuss the ubiquity of interpretation in everyday life, asserting that "interpretation is . . . perhaps the most basic act of human thinking; indeed, existing itself may be said to be a constant process of interpretation" (pp. 8–9). Virtually any act of meaning making or understanding is the result of interpretation. In fact, according to Palmer,

> interpretation is more encompassing than the linguistic world in which man lives, for even animals exist by interpreting. They sense the way they are placed in the world. A piece of food sitting before a chimpanzee, a dog, or a cat will be interpreted

by the animal in terms of his own needs and experiences. Birds know the signs that tell them to fly south. (p. 9)

When it comes to human beings, however, Palmer clarifies that "the phenomenon of language" (p. 9) must be dealt with, for

> language shapes man's seeing and his thought—both his conception of himself and his world (the two are not so separate as they seem). His very vision of reality is shaped by language. . . . If the matter is considered deeply it becomes apparent that language is the "medium" in which we live, and move, and have our being. (p. 9)

In addition to shaping thought and our vision of reality, Palmer (1969) suggests (referencing Gadamer) that language, by its nature, has a voice—that is its strongest modality of being. In interpreting a language-based text, therefore, the voice of the text must be heard in order to understand. Hearing the voice of the text is what allows understanding more so than conceptualizing or analyzing. This is because, according to Palmer's engagement with hermeneutics, understanding is more than an intellectual activity. It is, as he put it, "both an epistemological and an ontological phenomenon" (p. 10). Understanding a text is therefore an "encounter" (p. 10) between the person and the text. It is not "a scientific kind of knowing which flees away from existence into a world of concepts; it is an historical encounter which calls forth personal experience of being here in the world" (p. 10). Further, Gadamer's dialectical hermeneutics sees mutuality between the interpreter and the text. The text, once again, is not a fixed reality with an objective meaning but is rather a participant in a "fusion of horizons" (p. 208) between the text and the interpreter. This means that rather than becoming "master" of a text, one becomes the " 'servant' of the text; one does not so much try to observe and see what is in the text as to follow, participate in, and 'hear' what is said by the text" (p. 208). Palmer explains the encounter between the interpreter and the text in the hermeneutic experience according to Gadamer:

The method appropriate to the hermeneutical situation involving the interpreter and the text . . . is one that places him in an attitude of openness to be addressed by the tradition. The attitude is one of expectancy, of waiting for something to happen. He recognizes that he is not a knower seeking his object and taking possession of it—in this case, by coming to know "how it really was" or what the text "really meant," by trying to shake off his prejudices and see with a purely "open" mind. Rather, the methodical discipline is one designed to restrain his own will to master. He is not so much a knower as an experiencer; the encounter is not a conceptual grasping of something but an event in which a world opens itself up to him. Insofar as each interpreter stands in a new horizon, the event that comes to language in the hermeneutical experience is something new that emerges, something that did not exist before. In this event, grounded in linguisticality and made possible by the dialectical encounter with the meaning of the transmitted text, the hermeneutical experience finds its fulfillment. (p. 209)

For the current study, the "text" was the dialogue amongst the three bodies of literature. I situated myself within this exchange, listened in on the dialogue, and waited for the voices of the texts to emerge as a result of this exchange. As the interpreter, my job was as an "experiencer" and coparticipant in the "fusion of horizons" between the three bodies. In the hermeneutic interpretation of this dialogue, I was open to a "new vision of reality" that sought to emerge in the context of this conversation.

Although hermeneutics as a method or pathway into this study clearly addresses the presence of the researcher in the research process, it does not fully account for the depth psychological understanding of what the researcher brings to the work. The depth psychological understanding of the researcher acknowledges not only the conscious engagement of the researcher but also the unconscious engagement of the researcher with the work (Romanyshyn, 2007). The current study was undertaken as research relevant to clinical psychology and was informed by a Jungian perspective on the psyche and the unconscious. Therefore, in combination with the hermeneutic method, an imaginal approach, with its processes and method for making a place for the unconscious engagement of the researcher with the work, allowed for the more direct applicability of the findings to depth psychological research.

## The Imaginal Approach to Psychological Research

The imaginal approach to psychological research, as developed by Romanyshyn (2007) in *The Wounded Researcher: Research with Soul in Mind*, is an approach that makes room for the unconscious in the researcher during the research process. Romanyshyn explains in *The Wounded Researcher* that philosopher Henri Corbin used the term *imaginal* to "differentiate a region of reality that is intermediate between sense and intellect and that mediates between them" (p. 81). Citing the work of Jung and archetypal psychologist James Hillman, Romanyshyn identifies this intermediate region as "the world of soul" (p. 81). As a world between sense and intellect, the world of soul "has its own ontological status as a domain of reality between the domains of matter and mind" (p. 81). Romanyshyn argues that psychology and psychological research attend to this *world of soul* but can never entirely reveal all there is to know about the soul or about a particular piece of psychological research. This is so because every psychological tradition has its own perspective and thus necessarily defines a particular view on the given topic. Of course every tradition attempts to take as wide and comprehensive a perspective as possible on a given topic or on soul itself but, inevitably, something remains outside the scope of that perspective despite the deepest desire to be omniscient. That which falls outside the scope of a given perspective is that which remains unconscious to that perspective. The world of soul continues to carry that which remains unconscious. Romanyshyn's imaginal approach to research then, acknowledges and attends to the world of soul by explicitly making room for the unconscious in the researcher during the research process.

An imaginal approach to research recognizes the reciprocity between the researcher and the work, not only in the process of doing the work, but even more significantly, in the choosing of the research topic.

This means that although the researcher *seemingly* chooses the topic through a completely conscious, ego-directed process, on some level there is also an unconscious pull to the work, through the researcher's psychic wounding (Romanyshyn, 2007). That which has unconsciously called the researcher to the work (like a new lover enticing one into deeper and deeper engagement with the unstated promise of making all things right in the world), might have a somewhat different agenda for the work than that which the ego had identified as the purpose of the work. What appears, consciously, to the researcher as a promising topic, fulfilling all the requirements for an appropriate scope of work, also unconsciously draws the researcher to the topic, perhaps with the hope of healing the psychic wound. For those who might question whether this means that research using an imaginal approach is truly research with something to contribute to the field of psychology and not simply for the benefit of the researcher, Romanyshyn makes clear, "this does not mean . . . that research is therapy, or that it should be" (p. 136). It means rather, that although the personal element of being drawn to the work through one's own wounding plays a significant role in the research process, this is simply the starting point for entry into a deeper engagement with the work. With a Jungian understanding of the unconscious levels of the psyche, the unconscious of the individual continues beyond the individual, and is the point of connection with deeper levels of the collective unconscious (Stein, 1998). It is on these deeper levels of the unconscious that the work serves a purpose beyond the individual.

Thus, the psychic wound of the researcher is precisely that which prepares him or her for work on the chosen topic and constitutes the researcher's "complex, unconscious ties to the work" (Romanyshyn, 2007, p. 26). This makes research more than an academic endeavor. Research becomes vocation—calling the researcher to the work; it is a "hermeneutics of deep subjectivity" (p. 272).

## Engaging the Transference Field Between the Researcher and the Work

The procedures developed in *The Wounded Researcher* (Romanyshyn, 2007) for the imaginal approach to research allow the researcher to attend to the vocational draw to the work and to engage the transference field between the researcher and the work. Roma-nyshyn (2007) explains:

> There is in the research process that would keep soul in mind an awareness that a transference field exists between the researcher and his or her work as much as it exists between a therapist and a patient, a love and a beloved, a teacher and a student, a parent and a child, a writer and an editor, a reader and a work. Perhaps the most important aspect of an imaginal approach to research specifically acknowledges this dynamic field between the two and establishes procedures that attempt to make this unconscious field as conscious as possible. (pp. 135-136)

Just as in the therapeutic process where a transference field exists, so also in the imaginal research process where a transference field exists, a withdrawal of projection must eventually occur and the transference be acknowledged. However, the utility of the transference field, as in therapy, depends upon one's willingness to engage in that field.

## Opening a Space for the Work

The choice of a research topic, as previously stated, involves both the conscious, ego-directed process of decision-making as well as an unconscious pull to the work. Once the topic has been chosen, however, the ego would like to "master" the work, as Palmer (1969) discussed, and kill it in order to dissect it. In other words, for the purposes of a scholarly dissertation, from an egoic perspective, the research process would involve the traditional methods of analytical research utilizing intellectual capacities in their most formally trained guises. The research process would remain under the ego's control at all times. In an imaginal approach to research, however, the researcher enters the transference field, loosening the ego's grasp and making space to engage the unconscious aspects of the work. How then, under the scrutiny and control of the ego, does one enter the transference field?

Entering the transference field must begin in a state of openness and wonder (Romanyshyn, 2007), with the attitude of not knowing what the work is about. This is making use of what romantic poet John Keats called *negative capability*. Negative capability requires tolerating uncertainty, mystery, doubt, "without any irritable reaching after fact and reason" (as cited in Romanyshyn, 2007, p. 149). So, rather than seeking after the certainty of facts as the ego would have us do, entering into a negative capability loosens the ego's grasp and opens up "a space of possibility" (Romanyshyn, 2007, p. 137). In this space of possibility, the researcher has "made a place for allowing himself to be addressed by the unconscious" (p. 137). It is in this space—in this transference field, where the steps of the transference dialogues unfold and the researcher begins to let go of her conscious ties to the work in order to find out what the work itself is about, beyond her own personal wounding.

The transference dialogue stems from Jung's use of active imagination (Romanyshyn, 2007) to loosen the boundary between the conscious and the unconscious psyche. Jung's use of active imagination was a recognition of the autonomy of the psyche; this is central to the idea that the work in which the researcher is engaged is autonomous and therefore its own purpose albeit accessed through the wounds of the researcher. To illustrate, this is similar to the telling and retelling of myths by classical poets throughout the ages. The myth itself has its own autonomy and "calls" to be told and retold by the poets throughout the ages who feel compelled to render the myths according to their own creative engagement. Shakespearean plays, likewise, have been performed over and over again, retelling the story that wants to be retold, or revealing something about soul, through the artists who feel the pull to render the play according to their own engagement with it, and set in their own historical context. This is perhaps what makes a contemporary retelling of Richard III, for example, seem so relevant and engaging to audiences 400 years after it was written. Research then, when seen in this way, is a vehicle for accessing the work that lives on, has its own autonomy (p. 153), and wants to be told (or healed) again or more fully. Therefore, rather than dictating what the work is about from an ego-directed position, which dismisses the autonomy of the work, the researcher enters into the transference field between oneself and the work with the sense that one no longer knows what the work is about. Indeed, the transference space is created through this act of humble submission. One begins to wonder and to ask, "what is this work really about?" . . . With this question, one has carved out a space of possibility. One has carved out a potential space, an imaginal space, for the work. (pp. 136-137)

Following this crucial "act of humble submission" to the work is a specific process of bringing the unconscious into the work.

## Letting Go of the Work to Bring in the Unconscious

Romanyshyn (2007) discussed a specific, two-part process of letting go of the work in order to engage in the transference field. The first phase, a phase of reverie, eases one away from the conscious relation to the work and toward the "unconscious sense of the work" (p. 141). The second phase is conducting the transference dialogues themselves, which invites the unconscious aspects of the work more directly and more fully into the research process. Both the phase of reverie and the transference dialogues are ways of letting go of the egoic hold on the work and engaging in the transference field.

**Reverie.** The reverie is not something directed—it happens spontaneously or can happen following a memory, a sense of longing, some kind of yearning, or anything that triggers the dreamlike state of reverie. The reverie itself is "a kind of abduction" (Romanyshyn, 2007, p. 142) and happens of its own accord but, in the research process, must be attended to after it happens. For, "reveries hold the secrets of the work, secrets that the researcher does not yet know" (p. 143).

**The transference dialogues.** The next phase of the letting go process involves the transference dialogues. The five steps of the transference dialogues include setting the stage, invitations, waiting with hospitality, engaging the "others" in the work, and scholarly amplification. The dialogues involve imaginal play between the researcher and that which emerges from the unconscious. Romanyshyn (2007) explains that the dialogues are an invitation to play in [the] imaginal landscape . . . [which] is a landscape of Winnicottian transitional phenomena in which the differentiation between the researcher and the work, his or her separation from it, is mediated by the fantasies and reveries and images of the work that emerge within this landscape. (p. 137)

Therefore, the steps of the transference dialogues involve an imaginal process like planning for a visit from invited guests. In this way the imaginal approach brings greater dimension to the dialectical hermeneutics previously discussed. Rather than a two-way verbal dialogue between the researcher and the text, the transference dialogues are more like a theatrical performance in which one plays a part on stage. If dialectical hermeneutics is like the libretto for an opera, the transference dialogues are the full operatic production taking place in the imaginal realm. One does not just listen for the voices of the texts in order to dialogue with them, one also makes use of the imagination to see the interactions, to hear the voices, to feel the affective engagement, to play a part in the action, and to essentially lose oneself in the "story" of the work.

*Setting the stage.* The transference dialogue begins by setting the stage. This involves a "mood of reverie, the attitude of negative capability, and the gestures of hospitality" (Romanyshyn, 2007, p. 150). These are the practices of research with soul in mind and are used throughout the research process, just as empirical researchers use measurement and observation. During stage-setting, the researcher also employs a "willingness not to disbelieve" (p. 150) what surfaces in the dialogues.

*Invitations.* The second step is an invitation to the others in the work. This involves invoking the others in the work at the ever-deepening and ever-expanding levels of the unconscious. In invoking the others in the work, one asks whom the work serves. Sending out invitations is therefore a means of hearing from the unconscious from whichever level of the unconscious something has been left unsaid and "wants" to be heard. The researcher can begin this phase of the research by invoking the others in the work at any level but must be prepared to be hospitable to what shows itself from any of the four levels of the unconscious. On the personal level, this involves inviting the others in the work from within one's own family or personal ancestry. On the cultural-historical level it involves more likely a people, rather than individuals. On the collective-archetypal level, it involves possible "guides or ancestors" (Romanyshyn, 2007, p. 152) such as mythological or archetypal figures. Finally, on the ecocosmological level, it involves posing the questions as to whom the work serves and who has a voice in the work to other creatures, such as the animals, the plants, or even the mineral realm. At each level, the invitation is to those whose voices from the unconscious wait to be heard. In response to this invitation, what voices are heard, or what others in the work show themselves, are completely unknown at the start of the research proces. The invitations are always sent out, therefore, as an open question as to whom the work serves, rather than as a request for an appearance from a partic-ular individual, people, figure, or realm.

*Waiting with hospitality.* The third step of the transference dialogues involves waiting "with hospitality" (Romanyshyn, 2007, p. 140). The waiting required at this step is not simply a finger-tapping kind of waiting but a willingness to remain in negative capability and to be attentive to moods that settle in, to images that surface, to voices that make themselves heard, and even to "bodily sensations" (p. 156). Being receptive to these, rather than dismissing or ignoring them is an important part of this step.

*Engaging the others in the work.* The fourth step involves giving form to the *appearances* of the others in the work. Romanyshyn (2007) explains:

> To give form to the process, the images that appear or the moods that are evoked or the bodily sensations that are felt can be drawn, painted, sculpted, or written as dialogue between the research and the "others" in the work. (p. 158)

In order for dynamic engagement between the researcher and the unconscious aspects of the work, form must be given to the "others" in the work. Romanyshyn makes it clear in *The Wounded Researcher*, however, that the material gleaned from the transference dialogues and the others in the work is not the actual data for the research; rather, it deepens any data collected in the study by revealing some of what may have been outside the conscious, egoic perspective of the researcher.

Once form has been given to the "others" in the work the researcher must then step back and return to a more "critical" (Romanyshyn, 2007, p. 159) position in order to reflect upon how the forms produced are related to the work. In reflecting from a more critical position on the forms produced in the dialogues, a differentiation between what one brings to the work and the work itself is made more clear. This is where the conscious mind of the researcher engages in a dialectical hermeneutic with the contribution from the unconscious. In this way, the transference dialogues serve to "situate objectivity deep in subjectivity" (Romanyshyn, personal communication, June 20, 2012).

*Scholarly amplification.* The final step of the transference dialogues is then the scholarly amplification of the material produced in the previous steps. This involves more traditional scholarly research that follows up on what was produced in the transference dialogues. One amplifies the images or figures that present themselves in the transference dialogues by exploring associations, cultural connections, myths, symbols, or even current events, to find the relevance of the image or figure to the research topic. This is its own hermeneutic process of working with the material produced in the dialogues as artifacts of the unconscious. Similar to the work of an archaeologist, the researcher using transference dialogues uses scholarly research skills to identify and understand the meaning of that which has been produced by the unconscious. An archaeological artifact would be considered by an archaeologist from many different perspectives, such as anthropology, art history, linguistics, ethnography, and others in order to gain a rich and meaningful understanding of the object in its proper context. In this way we might say the archaeologist amplifies the artifact by finding out not only what it is and what are its functions, but also the meaning of the artifact within the context in which it was originally created. What does the artifact say about the person who created it, about the culture in which it was created, about the uses of the artifact, its significance in domestic routine, interpersonal relations, religious ritual, et cetera. Likewise, the psychological researcher using transference dialogues to gain access to the unconscious considers that which rises up from the unconscious from many different angles and perspectives in order to unearth its significance beyond the personal, individual imagination or intellect of the researcher. This is, once again, one of the ways in which the researcher differentiates between his or her own transference to the research topic and that which is revealing itself as an unconscious aspect of the work itself in the chosen research topic. In discussing the final step of the transference dialogues in *The Wounded Researcher*, Romanyshyn (2007) reminds us that "the imaginal approach and the transference dialogues do not replace scholarly modes of research— they add an important and neglected aspect to them" (p. 161).

## The Alchemical Hermeneutic Method

Evolving from the imaginal approach to research as discussed above, Romanyshyn (2007) introduces a hermeneutic method in *The Wounded Researcher* that includes a Jungian understanding of the unconscious. This method was developed as a supplement to the transference dialogues and a complement to more traditional research methods—not as a replacement (p. 259). As a method, in contrast to the philosophical hermeneutics as discussed by Palmer (1969), alchemical hermeneutics "is about making philosophical hermeneutics more psychologically aware" (p. 222). In this way, Romanyshyn suggests, alchemical hermeneutics might be considered "the offspring of the encounter between the tradition of hermeneutics and depth psychology" (p. 235).

As a method to be used alongside more traditional research methods, alchemical hermeneutics allows for the inclusion of other aspects of the researcher's unconscious not surfaced in the transference dialogues, which are beyond the researcher's complex ties to the work. Inclusion of these other aspects of the unconscious is one of the ways of attempting to differentiate clearly between the researcher's own wounding and the work itself. These other aspects include dreams, feelings, intuitions, bodily symptoms, and synchronicities "as expressions of a researcher's unconscious participation in the work" (Romanyshyn, 2007, p. 260). Romanyshyn explains:

> It is a means of making method more complete, more comprehensive in its service to soul, by making a place for those more

subtle ways of knowing too often marginalized by methods that do not take into account the unconscious presence of the researcher to his or her work. (pp. 259-260)

In *The Wounded Researcher*, Romanyshyn (2007) discusses the use of the term *alchemical* to describe the hermeneutic method that "makes room for those other aspects of how a researcher travels into his or her work" (p. 259). He gives several reasons for using the term *alchemical*, one of which is Jung's understanding of the unconscious and his work with alchemy as central to this choice of term. Romanyshyn sees the researcher as

alchemist in relation to his or her work . . . [in] a process of making and unmaking, of constructing the work from the ego's point of view and having it deconstructed from the soul's point of view, of holding onto a work by letting go of it. (p. 262)

In this way, alchemical hermeneutic research is, like alchemy, a transformative process of turning base matter into something much more valuable. The base matter would be the starting point of the ego's perspective on the work, and the more valuable result of the transformative process is the healing, albeit incomplete, of that which calls to be healed in and through the researcher. As Hermes promised, the whole truth is never told, the whole work is never completely done.

Alchemy itself, as understood by Jung and made accessible by von Franz (1980), was not simply about the transmutation of base matter into gold but is metaphorically about the process of psychological development. Because the alchemists considered themselves to be studying the "unknown phenomenon of matter" (p. 21), but had no "definite intention or tradition" (p. 21) in making their observations and interpretations, they entered their work from a stance of unknowing (meaning that the ego is not completely in charge) and made unconscious projections onto that which they observed. Their findings are replete with what Jung recognized were actually symbols from the unconscious; these symbols, said von Franz, metaphorically depict psychological processes. Further, alchemy is concerned with transmutation and transformation, which are key features of psychological growth and the individuation process, as well as the research process that would keep soul in mind (Romanyshyn, 2007). Therefore, the term *alchemical* signifies both the process of transmutation and transformation, and the embeddedness of the unconscious within this process.

Alchemical hermeneutics serves to deepen the hermeneutic circle and transform it into a "hermeneutic spiral" (Romanyshyn, 2007, p. 222) through an alchemical engagement of the researcher. This deepens "the relational aspect by making a place for those other subtle unconscious connections between a researcher and his or her work expressed in dreams, intuitions, feelings, symptoms, and synchronicities" (p. 222). The hermeneutic circle becomes a spiral as the mutuality between the researcher and the work is brought into play on conscious and unconscious levels. During the research process, engaging with the work in this way has the potential to transform the researcher during the course of research. This process of transformation, said Romanyshyn (2007), occurs when the researcher uses a deep subjectivity to both penetrate and be penetrated by the work itself. In so doing, at first a loss of differentiation between researcher and work occurs, to the extent that the researcher loses him or herself in the work, followed by a subsequent differentiation between what one brings to the work and the work itself.

In this way, alchemical hermeneutics alters our understanding of method and the relationship between the researcher and the work. In contrast once again to methods of research aiming toward objectivity via the separation between mind and body/subject and object, alchemical hermeneutics approaches from the perspective of subject-to-subject engagement via deep subjectivity. Romanyshyn (2007) makes clear that in this approach,

> we have moved from an understanding of method as a way into one's work, a way in which one knows a work to the degree that one is separate and distant from it, to method as a matter of intimate engagement, in which one knows the work to the degree that one *is* the work. (p. 272)

Thus, alchemical hermeneutics adds a dynamic dimension to the research process that allows for research with soul in mind. Through subjective participation in the research process, with acknowledgement of one's unconscious contribution rather than denial of it and awareness of the autonomy of the work that calls one to research, the world of soul—and the soul of the work, may be served.

## Ethical Considerations

In using a hermeneutic method, the parameters for the current study were defined by the chosen bodies of literature, rather than by a particular demographic population of research participants. Because no human participants or unpublished case material was used for this study, the ethical considerations were limited to the ethics of scholarship rather than ethics regarding the treatment of human beings for the purposes of the study. Alchemical hermeneutics, as a variation on traditional hermeneutic methods, added another dimension to the ethics of research. In so far as the imaginal approach to research, out of which the alchemical hermeneutic method arises, makes a place for the unconscious in the research process, this approach requires the researcher to become as conscious as possible of his or her unconscious ties to the work. Otherwise, the researcher is at risk of projecting unconscious complexes onto the research. The alchemical hermeneutic method therefore brings with it this additional ethical dimension regarding the unconscious into the research process.

## Reflexivity and Limitations of the Current Study

Literature on children's spirituality, self and sense of self development, and the human–nature connection delimited the current study. Due to the vastness of each of these bodies of literature, literature that lends itself to making connections between the three realms was selected for the sample literature. Thus in the section on children's spirituality, literature addressing the inner experience of the child was given priority over literature defining spirituality through measurable behaviors such as church attendance, performance in school, or receiving mental health services. In the section on self and sense of self development, literature was chosen based on its relevance to questions about the spiritual nature of the child and, in some cases, based on its potential for considering the human–nature relationship. In the section on the human–nature connection, once again, literature that focuses more on the inner experience of the child rather than behaviors was prioritized.

The limitations of the current study were therefore those imposed by its theoretical nature. In addition, the findings are presented from a perspective informed and shaped by the culture of Western, industrialized society in the 21st century. Whether these findings are applicable to people in other parts of the world remains to be seen. Further discussion of these limitations and how they might be rectified in an attempt to bring greater validity to the findings is found later in the study, in the chapter containing suggestions for future research.

## Organization of the Study

Following the current chapter on methodology is an overview of the literature that serves as a foundation and context for exploration of the topic. Because the autobiographical origins of my interest in the topic consisted initially of questions about the integration of spirituality and psychology, this overview explores representative literature and ideas from some of the major figures in early depth psychology. Thus the overview of literature in chapter 2 begins with the assertion that spirituality has been addressed in the field of depth psychology since the beginning.

The monumental work of William James provides a starting point for the overview of literature, both affirming this assertion and serving as a point of reference for the many contemporary pieces of literature later discussed. Following a summary of relevant points made by James in *The Varieties of Religious Experience* (2008), a brief encapsulation of Carl Jung's integration of spirituality into psychology, contrasted with Sigmund Freud's perspective on spirituality ensues. From there, an overview of some of the major contributors to the field of children's spirituality, including secular educators, religious educators, and psychologists, depicts the relatively late inclusion of spirituality in child and developmental psychology as well as the cross-pollination of ideas between the fields of psychology, theology, and education on the subject of children's spirituality. This overview is designed to generally highlight some of the relevant issues addressed on the topic of spirituality in psychology and more particularly on the topic of children's spirituality.

Following the overview is chapter 3, the formal review of literature relevant to the topic. This chapter has three main sections, each of which reviews literature from one of the three main aspects of the research question. These three sections are children's spirituality and spiritual development, self and sense of self development, and the human–nature connection.

Proceeding from the three sections in the review of the literature are chapters on each aspect of the research question: chapter 4 amplifies the literature on self and sense of self development, chapter 5 delves more deeply into the contemporary literature on children's spirituality and spiritual development and chapter 6 amplifies the literature on the human–nature connection, with particular emphasis on children in the natural world.

Chapter 7 presents a discussion of the methodology used in this study. The incorporation of the imaginal approach to research and the alchemical hermeneutic method utilized in this study is discussed and evaluated based on my experience in using them throughout the research process. This is elaborated by a depiction of the process of attending to the alchemical hermeneutic collection of dreams, symptoms, synchronicities, feelings, intuitions, and the impact they have on the work throughout the course of this study. Within this elaboration, my vocational and complex ties to the work are discussed.

Attending to these other expressions of the unconscious necessitated keeping a logbook throughout the process, documenting these contributions from the unconscious as they occurred. In excerpts from this logbook of transference to the work, I include resistances encountered throughout the process, as these are also valuable contributions from the unconscious. Finally, this chapter provides not just a summary of the impact of the unconscious on the work but also specific examples of how engagement with the unconscious dynamics of the work contributed to the alchemical transformation of the researcher and the work.

Chapter 8 then presents the results from the study and a theoretical depiction of the interpermeating (W. Adams, 1999) relationships between children's spirituality, sense of self, and the natural world. The results of the study are an integration of the contributions from the unconscious with the findings obtained in looking at the overlap and interplay between the three main bodies of literature.

Finally, chapter 9 provides a discussion of the implications of this study for depth psychology. In addition, I offer suggestions for empirical, participant-based studies that might shed light on some of the theoretical findings put forth in this study. The limitations of the study are also examined.

*Chapter Two*

# Where Spirituality and Psychology Meet

As stated previously, my interest in studying psychology began with questions about the relationship between psychology and spirituality. The course of events—or more precisely, the evolution of my thought process leading to the current study, was consistently permeated with consideration for the *boundaries of the soul* and how to conceptualize the spiritual nature of being human within psychology. When I began the research for the current study, my hope was to illuminate the substrate or soil from within which the current literature has grown. Parallel to identifying the autobiographical origins of interest in the topic, I sought to trace the history of interest in the topic within the field of psychology. This would provide a context for the current study and would perhaps offer an opportunity to revisit prior understandings with new eyes and ears, or from a different perspective. As I explored the literature on religion and spirituality within psychology, I found that the realm of depth psychology has held the question of this relationship and its meaning since its beginnings.

The following summation of significant pieces of literature and authors aims to situate the current study within a context broad enough to encompass all three aspects of the research question, starting with the question of how spirituality has been addressed in the psychological literature. How has this topic been addressed and what bearing does this have on the current study in its attempt to find the places of overlap between spirituality, sense of self, and the natural world? Is spirituality a psychological aspect of being human, a dimension of human experience, or are human beings spiritual by nature? When it comes to children's spirituality, how has this been addressed, in what context, and by whom? Have depth psychologists addressed the question of the spiritual nature of the child? Further, has sense of self been addressed in this literature? Has the human–nature relationship been addressed in this literature? These questions guided my investigation of the literature that provides a foundation for the current study.

## William James

Harvard University psychologist and philosopher William James (2008) is credited with being one of the first in the realm of psychology to take a look at the significance of religious experience in the individual. In 1900-1902, when he delivered his talks for the renowned Gifford Lecture series in Edinburgh, a great deal of excitement existed regarding the Darwinian theory of evolution. Evolutionary theory had a profound impact on the science of psychology (Hergenhahn, 2005), prompting psychologists to attempt an understanding of the human psyche within the schema of evolution. Through an evolutionary lens, the new science of psychology took up the study of the psychological significance of religion. The "survival-theory" (James, 2008, p. 362) postulated that religion and personal religious experience had evolved, like the physical and behavioral characteristics of human beings, as an aid to survival rather than for reasons purported by religion. It was within this Zeitgeist that James delivered lectures leading to what was to become his monumental work, *The Varieties of Religious Experience*, in 1902.

James (2008) began his lectures by differentiating the work of psychology from the work of religion. In his study of the religious experiences of exceptional individuals, he did not set out to determine the truth or untruth of religious doctrine but rather to explore the psychological basis of religious experience. His premise was that "if the inquiry be psychological, not religious institutions, but rather religious feelings and religious impulses must be its subject" (p.12).

James (2008) was the first in a tradition of psychological exploration of religious experience (or spirituality) to place emphasis on the personal, inner experience of the individual. This emphasis, he believed, would have a greater weight of truth than focusing on an exploration of universal truths of the psychology of religion. He asserted,

So long as we deal with the cosmic and the general, we deal

only with the symbols of reality, but as soon as we deal with private and personal phenomena as such, we deal with realities in the completest sense of the term. (p. 362)

Defending the impulse to explore the subject of religion from within the realm of psychology, James (2008) put forth his argument for the empirical study of personal religious experience. His particular empirical study valued the subjective, feeling experience of individuals, as recounted by those individuals, over and above "objective" and intellectual findings of scientific reality, which are based more on belief than on experience. This differentiation between the personal spiritual experience and the objective measurement of religious behavior continues in the literature today as psychologists, educators, and academics grapple with questions about the spiritual nature of human beings and how it plays a part in social and psychological functioning and individual development (Scarlett & Warren, 2010).

In addition to the emphasis on the importance of personal religious experience, another aspect of James's legacy to the study of spirituality was his identification and description of mystical states of consciousness as being the taproot of what he called religious experience but what would be referred to today as *spirituality*. In *The Varieties of Religious Experience*, James (2008) asserted that "personal religious experience has its root and centre in mystical states of consciousness" (p. 277). Acknowledging the limitations and confusion that accompany the term *mystical*, he clarified its meaning by outlining four characteristics of mystical states of consciousness: ineffability, noetic quality, transiency, and passivity (pp. 380-381). *Ineffability* indicates the indescribable nature of the experience, whereas *noetic quality* describes an unusual, spontaneous knowing that occurs in the mystical state. The noetic quality was defined by James as a state of "insight into depths of truth unplumbed by the discursive intellect" (p. 278). The characteristic of *transiency* simply acknowledges that these are passing states that differ from the individual's usual state. Finally, *passivity* describes the feeling of the individual in whom the mystical state of consciousness occurs; it comes about as if on its own, and the person experiencing it feels a loss of his or her own personal will.

James (2008) thus situated the psychology of religion in the realm of personal experience and identified mystical states of consciousness as the heart of that experience. He also identified *saintliness* as the end toward which these religious experiences occur. Recognizing that one may strive for sainthood and that in most cases, it is not obtainable, he expounded the benefit of progressing in the *direction* of saintliness. He stated that as a personal quality, "the saintly character is the character for which spiritual emotions are the habitual centre of the personal energy" (p. 202). In this way, the "saintly character" (p. 202) has much in common with what could be described simply as that of a person with a spiritual orientation to life. *Saintliness*, according to James entails four characteristics:

1. A feeling of being in a wider life than that of this world's selfish little interests; and a conviction, not merely intellectual, but as it were sensible, of the existence of an Ideal Power.
2. A sense of the friendly continuity of the ideal power with our own life, and a willing self-surrender to its control.
3. An immense elation and freedom, as the outlines of the confining selfhood melt down.
4. A shifting of the emotional centre towards loving and harmonious affections, towards "yes, yes," and away from "no," where the claims of the non-ego are concerned. (pp. 202-203)

In James's (2008) work, the question then becomes, why live a spiritual life? He concludes that "the pivot round which the religious life, as we have traced it, revolves, is the interest of the individual in his private personal destiny" (p. 356). This statement is significant to the current study in that it speaks to the centrality of the "religious life" (p. 356) to the trajectory of an individual's personal life. From this perspective, the spiritual serves a purpose in determining the ultimate outcome of the person's life and the fulfillment of who the person is to become. Although James does not speak of a *sense of self*, his articulation of the purpose of the religious life is closely related to questions of sense of self: who the person is to become and what the person is to experience and accomplish in life. A distinction can be made between *destiny*, which denotes some sort of divine determination of a person's life, and *sense of self*, which concerns who a person feels himself or herself to be and, based upon that perception, how that person's life unfolds. Although clearly not parallel in all aspects, both *destiny* and *sense of self* suggest some kind of essential truth about a person, one from the perspective of divine order and the other from the perspective of internal experience of oneself.

The vast majority of the materials reviewed for the current study make reference to James's (2008) seminal work on spirituality. *The Varieties of Religious Experience* seems to have established the empirical study of personal religious experience as a legitimate subject of psychological investigation. In the lectures, James denounced what was being put forth as an objective, scientific perspective on this topic for its dismissal of the reality of personal religious experience in favor of the survival theory paradigm of evolution as a way of understanding the practice of religion. According to Scarlet and Warren (2010), his conceptualization of mystical states of consciousness at the core of the religious experience has endured as one of the ways spirituality is discussed in contemporary literature. Furthermore, these authors noted that James's articulation of the religious life contains a *telos* or developmental endpoint. In the current developmental literature, this viewpoint is referred to as an *organismic* theory of development, which sees the religious life as functioning within the whole person or organism rather than as an isolated aspect of the person's life (pp. 642-643).

## Carl Jung and Sigmund Freud

Early in his career, analytical psychologist Carl Jung (1961/1989) had an interest in religion and the spiritual. As a medical student, he discovered spiritualist teachings from the 1870s, which were for him "the first accounts . . . of objective psychic phenomena" (p. 99). A few years later, he completed his doctoral dissertation entitled "On the Psychology and Pathology of So-Called Occult Phenomena in Psychiatric Studies" (1902/1970, pp. 3-88 [*CW* 1, paras. 1-150]). For Jung, the reality of the objective psyche or unconscious became the linchpin of his entire body of psychological work and is central to the current study on spirituality. Whereas his one-time mentor and friend, Sigmund Freud, laid the groundwork for the psychoanalytic school to move in the direction of atheism with a dismissal of religion as primitive wish-fulfillment (Freud, 1937/1967), Jung's work engaged with the question of religion in such a way as to open the door to the integration of spirituality and psychology.

Similar to James's (2008) differentiation between the existential and philosophical perspectives on religion, Jung (1938) was interested in an empirical and phenomenological investigation of the psychology of religion rather than evaluating the theological truth of religion or religious creed (pp. 2-3). While delivering the 1937 Terry Lectures at Yale University, in his opening remarks, Jung provided a matter-of-fact and logical justification for the study of religion in psychology:

> Since religion is incontestably one of the earliest and most universal activities of the human mind, it is self-evident that any kind of psychology which touches upon the psychological structure of human personality cannot avoid at least observing the fact that religion is not only a sociological or historical phenomenon, but also something of considerable personal concern to a great number of individuals. (p. 1)

Although this lecture series was delivered well after Jung had published many other essays and books, this statement is a compact and simplified depiction of his empirical approach to the investigation of the psyche. In this instance, he knowingly stated the obvious fact that religion has been and continues to be an activity of the human mind since time immemorial; he claimed this as an empirical, observable fact based on various forms of cultural artifacts, archeological evidence, and literary and historical documents. He undertakes a phenomenological approach that concerns itself "with occurrences, events, experiences, in a word, with facts" (Jung, 1938, p. 3). Although this perspective on what constitutes an empirical fact contrasts with the contemporary emphasis on quantitative measurement as the basis for empirical fact, it nonetheless couches his work in an evidentiary base, rather than in philosophical logic or metaphysical theory.

Rather than starting with a theory on intrapsychic functioning, such as Freud's drive theory (1927/1989), and framing the practice of religion within that model of functioning, Jung (1938) began with a functional model of the psyche that acknowledges the objective reality of the psyche and the autonomous nature of religious experience (p. 4). These two concepts are discussed later in the literature review, but in this brief overview of spirituality in psychology, it is important simply to note Jung's engagement with the phenomenon of religious experience in human psychology as a salient feature of his work. In contrast once again, Freud (1927/1989) used a reductive approach to address the question of religion, thus diminishing the significance and validity of religious practice and spirituality to a neurotic manifestation of the unresolved oedipal complex. In the lineage of Freudian psychoanalytic theory, religion and spirituality were left out of the picture almost entirely until relatively recently (Küng, 1978/1990).

## Abraham Maslow

Although James and Jung clearly recognized the relevance and significance of spirituality and religion in psychology, the field of psychology was dominated for roughly the first half of the 20th century by the Freudian psychoanalytic perspective on the one hand, and a behaviorist perspective on the other (Cunningham, 2012), neither of which focused on the question of religion or spirituality in psychology. This was until those who are known as the "third force" (p. 109) humanistic psychologists gave rise to a new perspective—one that attempted to understand the factors contributing to psychological health, rather than focusing primarily on pathology. Abraham Maslow was one of the key figures in this "third force" psychology. Stemming from his work, the human potential movement took shape, which in turn set the stage for transpersonal psychology, sometimes referred to as the "fourth force" (p. 110) in psychology. Maslow's own work continued into this fourth force psychology.

Maslow's (1987) focus on the factors contributing to healthy psychological development led him to a theory of motivation based on a hierarchy of human needs. The first level of this hierarchy includes the physiological needs for living, such as breathing, food, water, and sleep. Once these physiological needs are met, needs for safety and security may then be met, followed by social needs, esteem needs, and self-actualization needs. Simply put, the theory states that only when basic needs are met, can a person begin to work on meeting the higher-level needs. Thus someone who has no sense of safety and security has no motivation to fulfill social needs, or if esteem needs are not met, motivation to meet needs for self-actualization is lacking. When an individual is engaged with meeting the more basic needs and is therefore hindered in meeting the higher needs, Maslow (1999) called this "deficiency motivation" (p. 36). When, in contrast, a person has met basic needs, he or she reaches a different level of motivation which he called "metamotivation" (Maslow, 1971, p. 289). Maslow argued that when a person is motivated primarily by meeting deficiency needs, his or her perspective on reality is clouded by the motivation to meet these needs. Having basic needs met, however, results in a clearer perception of reality and a higher degree of freedom from the mandates of meeting basic needs.

Similar to James's reasoning on looking at the lives of extraordinary individuals to gain insight about religious experience, Maslow chose to look at the lives of self-actualized people in order to gain insight about what factors facilitated and contributed to their self-actualization. People who are self-actualizing have "the full use and exploitation of talents, capacities, potentialities, etc." (1987, p. 150) and they have "transcended the geographical limitation of the *self*" (Maslow, 1969, p. 4). These people are not primarily directed by deficiency motivation; they have had their needs for physical survival, for safety and security, for loving and belonging, and for esteem all met. These are people who have freedom from the demands of these needs and are then free to meet their full potential. As Maslow put it, "The fully developed (and very fortunate) human being, working under the best of conditions tends to be motivated by values which transcend his *self*" (p. 4).

Maslow (1969a) found that one of the characteristics differentiating self-actualizers from those motivated by deficiencies was what he called *peak experiences*, which he perceived as moments of acute awareness of transcending the self. In his article in the first publication of *The Journal of Transpersonal Psychology*, "The Farther Reaches of Human Nature", Maslow likened peak experiences to the experiences of religious mystics. Whereas, at the turn of the century James was careful to discuss religious experience in the context of religion, even identifying "saintliness" as the aim of religious experience, 60 years later Maslow discussed his notion of peak experiences, noting that "they have almost all the characteristics attributed to universal religious experience" but do not "necessarily [have] to do with one creed or another" and can happen "at any time, at any place, and to practically anyone" (p. 8).

In the same initial issue of *The Journal of Transpersonal Psychology*, Maslow (1969b) authored another article in which he described 35 meanings of transcendence. This article was entitled "Various Meanings of Transcendence" perhaps harkening back to James's (2008) *Varieties of Religious Experience*, published in 1902. In 1969, however, now into the "fourth force" in psychology where the scope of perspective goes beyond the individual to the transpersonal, Maslow (1969b) discussed peak experiences and transcendence in the context of humanistic psychology rather than nonsecular society. This simply highlights the continuation of the integration of spirituality in psychology starting with James and continuing with Jung, and identifies the trend away from religion-based spirituality to spirituality considered an essential aspect of human nature.

Based on this brief review, clearly, the question of the spiritual or religious life has been explored since the beginning in the realm of depth psychology. The work of both James and Jung serve as the headwaters of a lineage of work exploring the interrelation between spirituality and psychology. As is true in the work of these two monumental figures in the realm of psychology, pains were taken in subsequent works by Maslow and others to differentiate between the psychology of religion (and spirituality) and religion itself. Whereas James's (2008) seminal work regarded religion as the natural vehicle for religious experience, Jung's work explored the psychological phenomenon of what he termed the "religious function" of the psyche (1938, p. 3) and Maslow later discussed "religionizing or sacralizing all of life" (Maslow, 1969a, p. 8). James emphasized the significance of the personal religious experience in the living out of one's personal destiny; Jung sought to describe a model of the psyche that integrated the spiritual nature of human existence; and Maslow saw peak experiences as central to self-actualization. In the contemporary literature, James's work has certainly had influence on the conceptualization of children's spirituality. Maslow's work as well, has been significant in the discussion on children's spirituality. Jung's work, however, seems to have been almost entirely left out of the discussion. His model of the psyche and the role of spirituality within it have, potentially, much to contribute to the discussion.

## A Brief History of the Interest in Children's Spirituality

Before psychologists began seriously considering the role of spirituality in children, what had been written about the spiritual life of the child was primarily the work of educators in both secular and religious schools. A theoretical framework that diminished the significance and validity of religion influenced the culture of psychoanalytic psychologists; this meant that the majority of psychologists adhering to this Freudian perspective avoided the question of spirituality in both adulthood and childhood. Although Jungian and Adlerian psychologists had room for the inclusion of spirituality in the theoretical constructs guiding their clinical practice, the question of spirituality specifically in children remained largely unexplored in these two other dominant streams of depth psychology. Child analyst Erik Erikson, as a neo-Freudian, was an exception and his work with children did recognize the importance of religion and spirituality in his model of developmental stages. Erikson wrote about basic trust in the first stage of development as important for the acquisition of a religion-based faith (Forsythe, 1997). In the realm of developmental psychology, Swiss psychologist Jean Piaget's work laid a foundation on which subsequent theories, such as Kohlberg's stages of moral development and Fowler's stages of faith development, contributed to the accumulation of wisdom on the topic of children's spirituality. Until recently, however, the individuals most interested in a holistic perspective on children's development that included spirituality, were not psychologists but educators seeking to improve the quality of the children's educational experience and tap into children's highest potential. This brief history of the interest in children's spirituality highlights a sampling of significant work that has contributed to the current literature on children's spirituality and spiritual development.

**From the realm of education:**

*Maria Montessori and Rudolf Steiner.* Two prominent figures from the field of education that have contributed to the study of children's spirituality and spiritual development were Maria Montessori and Rudolf Steiner. Montessori and Steiner, born in 1870 and 1861 respectively, were contemporaries of Jung and developed their educational models in the same climate of scholarly emphasis on the natural sciences in which James (2008) delivered his lectures on *The Varieties of Religious Experience.* Both educators took a scientific approach to the development of their methods of education and both defined their own theories of human development that underpinned their educational methods (Montessori, 1936/1966, 1948; Steiner, 1968/1997). Montessori (1936/1966) and Steiner (1968/1997) also wrote about the spiritual life of the child and incorporated their spiritual perspectives into their educational philosophy and methodology.

In Montessori education, one of the fundamental ideas is that all human beings are born with a unique potential and that each person has some value for the whole of humanity (Montessori, 1989). One of the goals of this educational approach, therefore, is to create an environment within which each child can work toward the fulfillment of this unique potential, directed in his or her work by an *inner guide* (Montessori, 1989). If the child is working in optimum conditions, supported by the Montessori method, and able to work toward his or her potential, the resulting process of growth and development will reveal a more enlightened way of life than any adult could ever impose upon the child. This occurs because, according to Montessori (1989), the child is being guided by his or her God-given potential and whereas the potential comes from God and is defined by God, the fulfillment of these inner demands is far greater than the fulfillment of any external demands defined by educators or other adults. This perspective on individual growth and development is facilitated by a curriculum Montessori termed *cosmic education* (1989), which, simply put, invites the child to see the interconnectedness of life and to see that all things in the natural world have a purpose that contributes to the whole. Through work and experiences in the classroom, the stage is set for children to make the connections that allow them to see the interdependencies of life as we know it. In turn, a door opens within the child to ask, "What is my purpose and what will my contribution be?" The work of the inner guide is thus aided by the child's intellect, which has been informed through guided experience in the external world. Asking this question about one's purpose from within a fertile field of experience and understanding is one of the primary aims of this approach to education. Although Montessori education is often referred to as a method, it is actually more than just a method; it is a philosophy, a way of life, and ultimately a tool for the transformation of society with the aim of creating a peaceful world (Montessori, 1936/1966).

Montessori (1989) emphasized the importance of the child's natural wonder, curiosity, and imagination in motivating the exploration that leads to learning and eventually to the fulfillment of the child's potential. She noted that asking questions about oneself and one's purpose in a community—first in the classroom, then in the world, is a self-reflective activity central to the child's spiritual growth. Having a sense of connection and belonging within a community as well as a sense of one's own responsibility within that community are also aspects of a child's spiritual growth (Montessori, 1936/1966). Although Montessori's primary aim was the education of the child, the spiritual nature of the child was clearly a primary consideration in the educational process. Rather than relegating the spiritual life of the child to specific practices or religious ritual, the Montessori method integrates a spiritual perspective on the child into the curriculum and classroom community, fostering the spiritual growth of the child through education.

Steiner came from a more spiritual scholarly tradition than did Montessori and was informed in his perspective significantly by the scientific work of Goethe and the spiritualist teachings of Theosophy. In 1919, Steiner established a method of education that relies on teaching with a "penetrating knowledge of man" (1968/1997, p. 3). His method of education, which has been adapted in the Waldorf Schools throughout the world, was based upon spiritual understandings in what he termed the *anthroposophical* tradition, which held that there is more to life than earthly experience—namely, a spiritual life that both precedes and follows temporal earthly existence. His belief system was rooted in the idea that "the world is created in spirit and comes forth out of spirit" (p. 1) and regarded spirituality and religion as closely intertwined. Spiritual life has significance for more than just the individual human being, in Steiner's view; he saw the higher purpose of spirituality in its service to humanity as a whole. He asserted that the ultimate meaning of the spiritual life was in its ability to "lift us out of our solitary egoism and draw us into community with other human beings" (1968/1974, p. 24).

In Steiner's (1968/1997) view, the vehicle through which the spiritual life of human beings could most effectively permeate the fabric of society was education. Steiner believed that the key to furthering the evolution of civilization was to "bring spirituality into the souls of men through education" (p. 3).

Although Steiner and Montessori had somewhat different understandings of spirituality, they both regarded it as the most important and the most *meaningful* component of human development, based on the centrality of it in their theory of human development. This regard for spirituality differentiates their educational methods from those in the mainstream during the first half of the 20th century and continues to differentiate the character of some of the current day Montessori and Waldorf schools. It also marks the beginning of a perspective on the child that integrates spirituality. For Montessori, like Steiner, the most important outcome of the spiritual development of the child was fulfilling one's God-given potential or destiny. In doing so, the child had the potential to make his or her greatest contribution to society (Montessori, 1936/1966).

### From the realm of religion and religious education:

*Edward Robinson's study of childhood religious experience.* In 1969, zoologist and scholar of religions, Alister Hardy, founded the Religious Experience Research Unit (RERU) at the Manchester College at Oxford after delivering his own lectures in the Gifford Lecture Series, the same lecture series to which James contributed his thoughts on religious experience. While heading up RERU, Hardy collected accounts of religious experiences from several thousand adults. In 1977, this voluminous collection of adult accounts was reviewed by a succeeding director of the RERU, Edward Robinson, for experiences reported to have taken place in childhood. From this study of 500 accounts, Robinson (1983) wrote a book, *The Original Vision: A Study of the Religious Experience of Childhood.*

In his foreword to Robinson's book, Hardy (1983) called *The Original Vision* "the first detailed study to come from the research" (p. 4) of RERU. Robinson (1983) noted that when he began his study, his interest was in "how children think and feel, how they experience the world" (p. 11). His objective in doing the study was to contribute to the wisdom on religious education or, in other words, the process of spiritual growth. In the book, Robinson took issue with the developmentalist perspective on childhood, which emphasized a chronological path of development. This perspective, he said, basically defined childhood in relation to adulthood, with adulthood being the better, more advanced stage of human development. Robinson referred to childhood as "not just a chronological period, a developmental stage to be defined however roughly in years, separating infancy and adolescence . . . [but as] an element of the whole person" (p. 8) and added that "this childhood may continue to grow and develop with life" (p. 8). As a perspective on childhood, the significance of this distinction between a strictly chronological stage and one that sees childhood as an "element of the whole person" (p. 8) becomes clearer upon considering the impact and importance of early religious or spiritual experiences.

Based on his review of the accounts of childhood experiences, Robinson (1983) proposed the idea that children have an "original vision" (p. 16) that is a perspective on life closer to "reality" (p. 9) than the perspective of most adults who supposedly have the market on the nature of reality. The *original vision*, which, he stated, neither occurs nor develops cognitively, is a perspective that sees the unity and interconnectedness of all of life and the "harmony of all things" (p. 19). Further, this vision comes about of its own accord. (This echoes James's statement that the condition of passivity characterizes mystical experience.) Robinson asserted that " 'the original vision' of childhood is no mere imaginative fantasy but a form of *knowledge* and one that is essential to the development of mature understanding" (p. 16). The original vision itself does not necessarily grow over time; in other words, the concept might not be expanded with additional information, and the vision itself may stay exactly the same, but the individual's experience of it may change over time. As Robinson stated, there is often a dimension to our early experiences that we can only become fully conscious of (if at all) in later life, when we compare them with other forms of experience that lack that dimension; in childhood we may be wiser than we know. (p. 8)

One of Robinson's (1983) important contributions to the current study is a conceptualization of childhood that maintains the relevance of childhood spiritual experiences in adulthood. His work also contributes the idea that childhood spiritual experience is natural and "everyday." He contrasted his approach to James's approach of studying extraordinary individuals' religious experiences. He intentionally made the point that the religious experience of childhood is natural and that, in their childhood state, individuals have access to a "transcendental reality" (p. 40) that is a truer reality than that which may eventually develop later in life through cognitive acquisition of insight, information, and understanding. In addition, in terms of spiritual development, Robinson demonstrated through statements made by the subjects in his study, that continuity of experience is more important than progression (p. 41); thus, a linear model of development, such as the Piagetian-based theories of moral development by Kohlberg and faith development outlined by Fowler, is not necessarily the best model for understanding spiritual development. In Robinson's language, he finds more "circularity" (p. 42) to the process of spiritual development than linearity.

Another important point in Robinson's (1983) work is his separation of the spiritual experiences of childhood from the circumstances in which they occur. Although he acknowledged that he had not made a "specialized study" (p. 30) of the correlation between the experiences and their circumstances as documented by RERU, he asserted that it would take much to convince him that "the actual trigger [for the experience] has any diagnostic value" (p. 30). He made this assertion in his chapter entitled "Nature Mysticism" and then went on to provide three in-depth accounts of childhood experiences in nature that left each child with a "profound sense of mystery" (p. 31), according to the grown child's (adult) account. One of the most descriptive examples of a childhood experience that induced a profound state of mystery and helped the child "become the person he or she had it in him or her to become" (p. 34) is the account of a 63-year-old adult male (a management consultant and advisor on industrial relations), who recalled an experience he had when he was 5 or 6 years old:

> It was a calm, limpid summer morning and the early mist still lay in wispy wreaths among the valleys. The dew on the grass seemed to sparkle like iridescent jewels in the sunlight, and the shadows of the houses and trees seemed friendly and protective. In the heart of the child that I was there suddenly seemed to well up a deep and overwhelming sense of gratitude, a sense of unending peace and security which seemed to be part of the beauty of the morning, the love and protective living presence which included all that I had ever loved and yet was something much more. (as cited in Robinson, 1983, p. 33)

Regarding this passage, Robinson pointed out that for this person, the emphasis was on personal feeling and relationships. He highlighted the main themes from other accounts as well to demonstrate that each experience resulted in personal and particular significance for the person. He reiterated that although nature was the context for each of the accounts he included in this chapter, the fact that "the beauty of nature started it all off is *incidental* [emphasis added]" (p. 34). Robinson's conclusions based on the adult accounts of childhood spiritual experiences thus exclude the notion that the circumstances in which they occur holds any particular significance. Later in this study, this question of whether the context in which the experience occurs has any importance will be addressed with a distinctly different conclusion proposed.

Robinson's (1983) main objective in publishing the study in mid-1970s England was for the purpose of influencing the perspective on childhood in the context of education, which he argued had changed little in the 50 years prior. He clarified that he was concerned with "the capacity of childhood for a certain type of experience, and the impact on it of our traditional form of education" (p. 79).

*Fowler's theory of faith development.* From the field of theology and human development, James Fowler developed a theory of the stages of faith development modeled after Piaget's stages of cognitive development (Parker, 2006). Fowler differentiated between faith itself and the constructs that serve to define the stages in the process of faith development. According to Stephen Parker, who reviewed Fowler's theory, Fowler claimed that faith is "a way of knowing, a way of constituting one's experience of the world" (2006, p. 337). Parker noted that the structures that define Fowler's theory on the stages of faith development and that "give shape to how humans construe and relate to self and the world" (p. 337) are a combination of Piaget's cognitive model and Kohlberg's model of moral stages of development, to which Fowler added the notion of a progression in one's "locus of authority" (p. 337). Fowler's model embraces the interconnectedness of these constructs and recognizes that moving through the stages "involves movement toward greater complexity and comprehensiveness in each of these structural aspects" (p. 337). Fowler's theory of faith development is another oft-cited source in the current literature on children's spirituality (e.g., Hay & Nye, 2006; McAdams, 1993; Newberg & Newberg, 2006; Ratcliff & Nye, 2006; Roehlkepartain, King, Wagener, Benson, & 2006a).

### From the realm of psychology:

*Kohlberg's model of moral development.* Kohlberg's model of moral development, which he developed from the late 1950s to the 1980s, was built upon Piaget's stages of cognitive development. His model consists of seven stages, with the seventh stage being beyond moral reasoning, which Kohlberg considered a postrepresentational stage of cosmic consciousness (Nidich, Nidich, & Alexander, 2000). According to Kohlberg's cosmic perspective in the seventh stage of development, the self and the universe are united" (p. 221). Clearly, this theory of moral development has contributed much to the exploration of spirituality in children (Walker & Reimer, 2006); however, Kohlberg's model relies heavily on the stages of cognitive development, as mentioned earlier. The more inclusive spiritual perspective on development would not limit the experience of the spiritual to only the highest states of consciousness. Spiritual development finds spirituality at all stages of the developmental process and manifests itself in ways other than just cognitively (Hart, 2003).

*Robert Coles's research on the spiritual life of children.* In 1990, psychoanalytic psychiatrist Robert Coles (1990) published *The Spiritual Life of Children*. According to a search of the PsychInfo database, since the publication of *The Spiritual Life of Children* in 1990 until 2011, 40 scholarly publications have included the terms *spiritual* and *children* in their titles. In contrast, articles on spirituality in adults during the same time period number close to 3,000. Half of the publications on children occurred between 2006 and June of 2011. Previously, between 2000 and 2005, 11 such titles were published; between 1995 and 2000, four; and between 1990 and 1994, five; thus, the interest in children's spirituality within the realm of the social sciences has steadily increased since Coles's work was published. A number of these publications, which include articles in academic journals, dissertations, and books, address spirituality as it relates to grief, coping skills, illness, and physical health. The remaining articles actually address spirituality itself. Based on this review of the database, people are increasingly interested in understanding not only the spiritual life of children but also the ways it might contribute to meeting the extraordinary circumstances of life, such as the death of a loved one, abuse, or childhood illness.

Coles (1990) spent 30 years working with and writing about children in the United States and other parts of the world before writing *The Spiritual Life of Children*. He worked with child psychoanalysts Anna Freud and Erik Erikson and has published numerous works on the inner life of the child. He recounted his early experience in training as a psychoanalyst in the late 1950s and early 1960s, when the question of a child's spirituality was not a part of psychoanalytic case conceptualization. He recalled his befuddlement when, after presenting an "ambitious psychoanalytic formulation" (p. 14) of a child with whom he had been working, his supervisor responded with what Coles thought was a completely irrelevant question: "Do you think she has her own religious ideas?" (p. 15). At that point in his training and in the realm of pediatric psychiatry, the question of religion or spirituality as part of the psychological picture of the child was missing. Over 30 years later, as Coles was writing *The Spiritual Life of Children*, he recalled his early awakening to the idea that the child might be able to teach him about his or her spiritual life if he was willing to put aside a pathologizing perspective and listen to the voice of the child. This was a shift that opened up a whole new world to Coles.

In *The Spiritual Life of Childrenr*, Coles (1990) narrated his own story of discovery of children's spiritual lives interwoven with depictions of moving and enlightening interviews with many different kinds of children from various religions, who were showing him and telling him about their spiritual lives. While he was still working with the girl who had been the catalyst for the shift in his perspective, Coles began to understand that there was a difference, for the child, between religion and spirituality. He observed that although this girl was a deeply religious 8-year-old raised in the Catholic tradition, "there was a personal, *spiritual* life in her that was by no means to be equated with her *religious* life" (p. 14). This distinction between religion and spirituality eventually became the focus for the 5-year study that resulted in his groundbreaking book.

In his book, Coles (1990) demonstrated the idea that spirituality in children is part of an integrated whole and is interwoven with all aspects of the child's inner life. As he stated, "the entire range of children's mental life can and does connect with their religious and spiritual thinking" (p. 108). He found that regardless of the religion to which a child belongs, spirituality helps children make sense of their experiences and define a meaning and purpose for their lives. Spirituality also helps children with emotional stability and assists in helping them to foster moral attitudes and to comprehend the mysterious or the ineffable. He found that children ask the same, age-old questions that adults have been asking seemingly forever: "Where do we come from? What are we? Where are we going?" (p. 37).

Regarding the relationship between children's spirituality and children's psychology, Coles (1990) asserted the existence of "a fusion" (p. 128), wonderfully depicted by a young girl who explained, "God is in heaven, but he is in my mind, too" (p. 128). He noted that children "construct" (p. 119) God within their inner lives and not necessarily according to the religious teachings they have been given, if they have even been given any. He stated,

> Psychologically, God can take almost any shape for children. He can be a friend or a potential enemy; an admirer or a critic;

an ally or an interference; a source of encouragement or a source of anxiety, fear, even panic. Obviously, religious tenets, reinforcing a child's ongoing spiritual reflection, can become an integral and persuasive part of a conscience, either its self-critical side or its friendlier aspect, the so-called ego-ideal of psychoanalytic theory. Often children whose sternly Christian, Jewish, or Moslem parents don't hesitate to threaten them with the most severe of religious strictures (and thus who do likewise with respect to themselves), can construct in their thoughts or dreams a God who is exemplary yet lenient, forgiving, encouraging, capable of confessing a moment's weakness or exhaustion now and then. (p. 119)

Throughout *The Spiritual Life of Children*, Coles (1990) invited the reader, along with him in his many interviews and interactions with children to experience the spirituality that is an integral part of children's lives. Rather than setting out to come up with a theory of children's spirituality or to operationaliz the spiritual life of the child, Coles engaged with the children on the topic of spirituality in an exploratory manner in order to learn from them. In his book, the child is ever-present and comes to life during the reading. As a qualitative piece of work, it provides a rich and penetrating perspective on the inner, spiritual life of young people. As far as spiritual development, based on his research, Coles acknowledged that children progress through stages of moral and faith development and reasoned that they surely progress in their "puzzling over" spiritual and religious matters, but he did not attempt to tackle the question of spiritual development. His contribution, which is particularly relevant to the study of the nature of children's spirituality, is therefore his encouragement to acknowledge and value the spiritual life of the child.

Evident in this brief history of the interest in children's spirituality, this topic was not addressed in the realm of psychology until relatively recently. Before there was interest in children's spirituality within psychology, the question of children's spirituality was left primarily to educators and religious education. The foundational works reviewed on children's spirituality by Robinson (1983), Kohlberg, Fowler (2006), and Coles (1990) bring forward several major, salient points to be explored further in the literature review. The nature of childhood spiritual experiences and their effect on the individual's development were addressed by Robinson and Coles, whereas Fowler and Kohlberg addressed two of the features of children's spirituality discussed in the contemporary literature: faith and morality. All of these authors spoke to the fundamental questions scholars continue to address in the literature: what does "spiritual" mean? What exactly are we attempting to address when we explore children's spirituality? What are children's spiritual experiences like? How are children affected by these experiences? Ultimately, what is it all for?

*Chapter Three*

# Creating a Context:
# A Literature Review

For the purposes of the current study, the relevant contemporary literature falls into three main categories: (a) current literature on children's spirituality and spiritual development; (b) self and sense of self development; and (c) the human–nature connection. This review provides relevant samples of literature addressing these main realms. It also investigates available literature that speaks to the overlap between all pairings of these three main categories; in other words, literature that addresses sense of self development and spirituality, then literature on spirituality and the human–nature connection, followed by literature on the human–nature connection and sense of self development. Finally, the review explores any available literature that addresses the relationship between these three main components of the current study.

Literature is reviewed primarily from six major domains: children's spirituality, developmental psychology, analytical (Jungian) psychology, psychoanalytic psychology, literature on children and the natural world, and ecopsychology. Analytical psychology has been chosen for its direct explication of, and relevance to all three of the main components of the topic. The other domains of literature have been chosen simply based on the availability and relevance of literature on the topic. The review of material from these domains will shed light on how prominent scholars in the field conceptualize children's spirituality and whether they are conceptualizing within a model of the psyche. Because there is no current research on children and the relationship between all three components of this study—spirituality, sense of self, and the human–nature connection—the review has been constructed to facilitate the exploration of, first, whether such a relationship exists and if so, the nature of that relationship.

## Review of Current Literature on Children's Spirituality

**Clarification of terms:** *Spirituality* **versus** *religion* **and** *religiousness.* To begin the review of the literature on children's spirituality, it is necessary to clarify some of the terminology used in the discussion amongst scholars on the topic. One of the most important points of potential semantic confusion occurs in the use of the terms *religion, religiousness, spiritual,* and *spirituality.* The connotations and perhaps even denotations of these terms has evolved over time and the terms have been used somewhat inconsistently in the literature. The evolution of these terms in the literature reviewed for this study seems to have occurred in conjunction with the evolving relationship between the church and the state. In searches on the topic of children's spirituality, authors from the United States, England, and Australia have written most of the literature. As the cultural (as opposed to political) relationship between church and state has evolved in these countries, the literature reflects greater differentiation between spirituality and religion. David Hay (2006) wrote a very clear chronicle of one segment of this evolution, its impact on education, and its societal implications for England in the first chapter of *The Spirit of the Child.* Although it is not the focus of this study to examine this evolving relationship, it is important to note that over time the collective understanding of spirituality has become more and more differentiated from the context of religion.

At an earlier point in time in the work of authors such as James (2008), religion was seen as an essential—or even mandatory vehicle for developing one's spiritual life. Spirituality was considered inextricably linked with religion, and although there may have been other purposes for the practice of religion both on the individual and societal levels, what is most relevant to this study is the historic view that religion offered a necessary, structured approach to fostering spirituality (James, 2008). *Religiousness* had more of the connotations of what we would call today *spirituality.* The concepts of spirituality and religiousness were intertwined and considered to be aspects of a person's religious development. James's (2008) work, *The Varieties of Religious Experience*, is a clear example of this cohesion between religion and spirituality, reflecting the cultural context in which he wrote. Over time, however, religion itself became associated with beliefs and practices as well as codes of morality, while spirituality became associated with one's subjective experience of that which was being fostered by religion (Roehlkepartain et al., 2006, p. 4). The term *religiousness* therefore now has connotations of adherence to religion—the beliefs and practices associated with a particular religion; the term *spirituality* on the other hand, has connotations of a human characteristic or quality not dependent upon religion for its inherent existence or lifelong cultivation (Roehlkepartain, et al., 2006). What we now call "spirituality" has become differentiated from the practice of religion and is considered to be something that may be cultivated through means other than religion, either, in some cases, as a substitute or in conjunction with the practice of religion (Hay & Nye, 2006). Simply put for the purposes of the current study, spirituality is distinct from religiousness and is not dependent upon religion for its cultivation.

In many of the scholarly chapters or articles, acknowledgement is also made of the distinction between an operationalized definition of spirituality for the purposes of psychological investigation and definitions that might be more accurate theologically (Newberg & Newberg, 2006). From James (2008) and Jung (1938) to contemporary authors on the psychology of religion, the distinction is made not just between a *theological* definition of spirituality and a *psychological* definition of spirituality but also between religion itself and religion from a psychological perspective. Hood, Hill, and Spilka (2009) stated, "Psychologists of religion do not study religion per se; they study people in relation to their faith, and examine how this faith may influence other facets of their lives" (p. 4).

**Definitions of childhood spirituality.** As spirituality has become more clearly differentiated from religion and religiousness, consideration for the spiritual life of the child has increased significantly in the scholarly literature. The "burgeoning of scholarly interest" (Roehlkepartain et al., 2006b, p. xiii) was noted in the editors' preface to *The Handbook of Spiritual Development in Childhood and Adolescence*. It is quite clear that children's spirituality is being recognized as relevant to overall growth and development, as evidenced not only by the increasing research but also by its inclusion for the very first time in a major developmental textbook, published in 2010 (Lerner, Lamb, & Freund, 2010). Therefore, what was until quite recently largely neglected in the developmental psychological literature (Hart, 2003; Roehlkepartain et al., 2006a) has now become a topic of primary interest for many scholars within the field. This has resulted in a rich and ongoing interdisciplinary discussion of the topic amongst psychologists, educators, and others, reflecting the relevance of the topic to many aspects of human life, and to many academic disciplines (Roehlkepartain et al., 2006, p. 3).

From a review of the relevant literature, two important broad generalizations about the nature of children's spirituality have emerged. First, the literature shows a fairly wide consensus at this point that spirituality in children is innate (Hart, 2003; Hay & Nye, 2006; Hyde, 2008; Myers, 1997). Second, it shows that spirituality is not dependent upon religion, religious schooling, or religious involvement, but rather is a dimension of the child's being before and beyond the question of religion (Hart, 2003; Hay & Nye, 2006; Hyde, 2008; Myers, 1997). Beyond these two premises, the seminal works on this topic depict many different ways of conceptualizing spirituality itself and, as yet there is no definitive consensus on the meaning of the term *spirituality*. As psychologist, author, and scholar of children's spirituality, Tobin Hart (2003), put it,

> defining [spirituality] is a bit like trying to hold water in our hands. We can hold some for a while and we may even bring some to our mouth and swallow, but a great deal just passes through unconfined, ungrasped. (p. 7)

Therefore, in order to allow for the scientific investigation of questions involving the subject of spirituality, written works typically contain a brief definition of spirituality given as a point of clarification at the start of the work, such as Newberg and Newberg's (2006) definition in a chapter on the neuropsychology of spiritual development: "Spirituality is usually regarded as less institutionally based and as more encompassing and inclusive of all groups and cultures than religiousness. Spirituality is also used to describe individual experiences such as those of transcendence and meaningfulness" (p. 183).

Other definitions of spirituality include spirituality as a search for the sacred—"a process through which people seek to discourse, hold on to and, when necessary, transform whatever they hold sacred in their lives" (Hill & Pargament, as cited in Roehlkepartain et al., 2006, p. 5)—and "one's engagement with that which she or he considers holy, divine, or beyond the material world" (Miller & Thoresen, as cited in Roehlkepartain et al., 2006, p. 5). Developmental psychologists Scarlett and Warren (2010) define spirituality as the "phenomenon of subordinating the self to something considered to be sacred" (p. 638).

The definitions above help orient the current study to the psychological realm intended for exploration; that is, the individual's experience and engagement with something beyond the self—the sacred or divine. More specifically, what and how the individual experiences and engages with the sacred or divine. What is it about human nature that describes or characterizes this engagement? How does this engagement affect the sense of self?

**Characteristics of children's spirituality.** From the sampling of literature reviewed, children are said to be innately spiritual and not only capable of having spiritual experiences in childhood, but apt to do so (Hart, 2003; Hay & Nye, 2006; Hyde, 2008; Myers, 1997). It is also broadly recognized in the literature that spirituality is distinct from religiousness; although there might be a relationship between spirituality and religiousness in a given person, spirituality is not dependent upon religion for its nurturance, cultivation, or development (Hart, 2003; Hay & Nye, 2006; Hyde, 2008; Myers, 1997).

In exploring children's spirituality, the authors reviewed tended to use not only descriptive terms to describe what children's spirituality is like but also functional terms to describe what it does—its action, as well as content terms to get at what it is within the child. Thus, children's spirituality is described as being relational and innate (Hart, 2003; Hay & Nye, 2006 Myers, 1997). Its function or activity involves transcendence, the subordination of the self to the sacred, movement toward ultimate unity, making meaning, integrating the self, and spiritual questing (Hyde, 2008). Spirituality is written about as a worldview, a set of capacities, such as the capacities for wonder, wisdom, wondering, relating, seeing the invisible (Hart, 2003), and as a set of awarenesses or sensitivities, such as awareness sensing, mystery sensing, and value sensing (Hay & Nye, 2006). Both Hart (2003) and Myers (1997) highlighted not only the relational nature of children's spirituality but its specific role in the spiritual development of adults who engage with children on a spiritual level. Hay and Nye (2006) also recognized the spiritual endeavor involved in researching children's spirituality.

While searching for an understanding of the nature of children's spirituality, authors, beginning with Coles (1990), also frequently noted the unique interaction between this dimension and the child's personal psychological makeup. In addition, early childhood spiritual experiences were noted to have significant lifelong relevance and impact on the individual. Hart (2003) discussed the notion that when children's spiritual capacities are nurtured, this results in a spiritual "temperament" (p. 10) or "world view" (p. 9) allowing integration of the child's personal life experiences with a perspective that seeks meaning and purpose in one's life as well as a connection with the sacred or divine. He also called spirituality itself a "process of development" (p. 9), which leads to the next area to be covered in this literature review.

**Childhood spiritual development.** Although, as noted, there has been an increase in scholarly writing about children's spirituality and spiritual development during the past two decades, it was not until 2006 that the first major collection of essays designed to further the field of spiritual development was published. At that time, the subject was still not considered to be in mainstream academia. Benson (2006), a leader in the field of children's spirituality, noted in his chapter from this volume that, "this field of study is still marginalized in the academy" (p. 484). Efforts have been made by many of the leaders in the field to bring attention to the importance of this topic in understanding the complete picture of child development. Particularly with adolescents, investigations have been conducted to understand the role of spirituality in what has been called Positive Youth Development (PYD) (Lerner, Roesner, & Phelps, 2008), which examines, from a psychological standpoint, how to help adolescents thrive. Many authors have promoted spiritual development as a central consideration in the life of the child and adolescent, such as

Roehlkepartain et al. (2006) in the opening chapter of *The Handbook of Spiritual Development in Childhood and Adolescence*:

> There is a core and universal dynamic in human development that deserves to be moved to center stage in the developmental sciences, alongside and integrated with the other well-known streams of development: cognitive, social, emotional, and moral. The name commonly given to this dimension is spiritual development. And it is hypothesized to be a developmental wellspring out of which emerges the pursuit of meaning, connectedness to others and the sacred, purpose, and contributions, each and all of which can be addressed by religion or other systems of ideas and belief. (p. 5)

Because this is a relatively new topic of academic study, though, historically, the question of our spiritual nature as human beings is age-old, the field is both vast and, in some respects, uncharted. Much of what we consider as part of our knowledge base about spirituality comes from the age-old, philosophical and theological explorations of the human condition; in more contemporary academia, however, the question of religiousness and spirituality has been explored anew from the perspective of the social sciences. Therefore, what we may have thought we knew from a theological or philosophical perspective becomes unknown once again, not only because of the nature of the subject matter but because of the challenge of articulating some of the same ideas from a new perspective.

Although it is acknowledged that operationalizing spirituality is antithetical to the nature of the topic, being that the term points to something ineffable, largely unknown, and unknowable, many scholars have made reference to a working definition of spiritual development. One definition crafted in 2003 by Benson, Roehlkepartain, and Rude, and cited in the first chapter of *The Handbook of Spiritual Development in Childhood and Adolescence* (Roehlkepartain et al., 2006a), states,

> Spiritual development is the process of growing the intrinsic human capacity for self-transcendence, in which the self is

embedded in something greater than the self, including the sacred. It is the developmental "engine" that propels the search for connectedness, meaning, purpose, and contribution. It is shaped both within and outside of religious traditions, beliefs, and practices. (Benson et al., 2003, pp. 205-206)

Much of what is attributed to spiritual development in this definition has been discussed previously as characteristic of spirituality in children, such as self-transcendence, meaning-making, and connectedness; however, what this working definition adds to an understanding of the current topic is consideration of life purpose and contribution to society. These were addressed explicitly in the works of Montessori (1936/1966) and Steiner (1968/1997), as well as James (2008) who wrote about the fulfillment of spiritual purpose or destiny as having meaning and significance beyond the life of the individual; the essential value of this fulfillment is in its contribution to the whole of humanity. Thus self-transcendence seen from this perspective is not limited to the spiritual life of the individual—her own spiritual experience and development, but is the entry point for sacred contribution to the whole.

In the foreword to *Positive Youth Development and Spirituality* (Lerner et al., 2008), Benson (2008) offered another perspective on spiritual development highlighting the interplay between the inner life of the child and the child's engagement with the world around her:

Spirit is an intrinsic, animating force that gives energy and momentum to human life. It also propels us to look inward to create and re-create a link between "my life" and "all life." Spiritual development, then, is a constant, active and ongoing process to create and re-create harmony between the "discoveries" about the self and the "discoveries" about the nature of life-writ-large. The two journeys (inner and outer) constantly inform each other and are always brought back into balance. (pp. viii-ix)

Benson drew attention to the shared "essence" of self and life, which was articulated by Hart (2003) in a slightly different tone.

Hart's explanation of a spiritual worldview stated, "all things, including us, are sacred and are infused with or part of spirit" (Hart, 2003, p. 9). Hyde (2008) also drew attention to the interplay and consistency between the self and the sacred with his statement: "At the centre of each individual's Self, then, is the Divine presence" (p. 38). Benson's (2008) definition of spiritual development above brought to the fore the idea that part of the child's process of spiritual development entails gaining awareness of this spiritual aspect of being—that the self (or the person) is one with something greater. At later stages of spiritual development, not only does this come into conscious awareness but has potential to be experienced as union with the divine. Hyde (2008) explained: "The notion of connectedness, or relationality, implies two objects being in relationship or connected to each other. Ultimate Unity, however, implies one. It entails the individual becoming one with Other" (p. 43). He then elaborated on how, according to Eastern philosophical perspectives, the individual gets to the point of experiencing Ultimate Unity: "The means by which Ultimate Unity may be attained involves the successive unfolding of higher levels of consciousness, which may enable the individual to transcend the ego in order to realize the true Self which is unified with Other" (p. 43). Hyde used the term *ego* in this explanation where other authors have used the term *self*, for example, in the "self-transcendence" Benson et al. (2003) included in their definition of spiritual development included above. Hyde (2008) also used the uppercase 'S' in *Self*, which has its own definition distinct from *self*. This is a potential point of confusion that will be clarified in the upcoming section of the literature review on Self and Sense of Self Development. Nonetheless, the above quote identifies not only ego-transcendence but "unfolding of higher levels of consciousness" (p. 43) as instrumental in realizing Ultimate Unity and therefore a part of the process of spiritual development, according to Hyde.

Hart's (2003) explanation of spirituality as an ongoing growth process addressed similar issues identified in Benson et al.'s (2003) definition of *spiritual development*, however, he did not use the phrase spiritual development. This reflects the perspective Hart (2003) took in *The Secret Spiritual World of Children* that sees life itself as spiritual. Indeed, Hart stated,

> Our life *is* a spiritual life. It is not that some of us are spiritual
> and some are not; our entire existence is a spiritual event, . . .
> a process of identity, of finding out more about who we really
> are. . . . It is also recognized as integration and wholeness; the
> more of ourself and the world we can integrate into our being,
> the greater our development. (pp. 8-10)

Rather than writing about spiritual development as a "dimension"
of development, Hart explicitly wrote about spiritual growth as the
whole point of existence, citing spiritual traditions and the world religions as support for this viewpoint.

Similar to Coles (1990), Hart's (2003) work allowed for the presence of the child to be experienced by the reader through the stories
told in the voices of the children themselves. Ratcliff and Nye (2006)
pointed out the need for this type of work emphasizing children's
experiences in order to better understand children's spirituality. They
remarked: "researchers have generally ignored children's own experiences . . . [and] rarely are children quoted" (p. 478) in child development textbooks. Despite this admonishment, one of the most current
developmental textbooks which includes a chapter on religious and
spiritual development continues to exclude the voices of children
themselves in the articulation of the most current theories. Scarlett
and Warren's (2010) chapter in the textbook *The Handbook of Life-
Span Development* (Lerner et al., 2010) does, however, offer a thorough academic overview of current research on religious and spiritual
development with an analysis of how the topic is being investigated by
researchers in the field.

Scarlett and Warren's (2010) work makes an important distinction between studies that use "belief-institution" conceptualizations of
spirituality and "faith-tradition" conceptualizations of spirituality. The
"faith-tradition" conceptualization allows for the inner experience of the
child, whereas the belief-institution concept focuses more on measurable behaviors and religious beliefs as in studies on religious-spiritual
development. The inner experience of the child is of greater import for
the current study due to its direct relevance to sense of self.

Finally, the Center for Spiritual Development in Childhood and
Adolescence at Search Institute launched a global initiative in 2006 to

establish better understanding of spiritual development and its relation to other aspects of development. In 2008, the Center published
a preliminary theoretical framework for spiritual development. This
framework identified three core developmental processes involved
in a "constant, ongoing, dynamic, and sometimes difficult interplay"
(Roehlkepartain, Benson, Scales, Kimball, & King, 2008, p. 40). The
three core processes in this interplay are awareness or awakening,
interconnecting and belonging, and a way of living. The cultivation
of meaning and purpose were identified as the thrust of the first two
of these developmental processes. The third, a way of living, entails
living life true to oneself with a spiritual orientation and connection to
the transcendent or divine. Spiritual development, according to these
researchers is a core developmental process for all persons that can be
recognized in "multiple expressions and experiences, including [those
of] young people who do not see spirituality as part of their identity
and worldview" (p. 54.).

## Review of the Literature on Children's Spirituality and Sense of Self Development

The review of literature on children's spirituality contained scant
examination of how spirituality contributes to the development of
a sense of self. Fowler's (1981) theory of faith development does,
however, make a contribution to this discussion even though he was
not specifically addressing this question. Faith, as an essential feature
of spirituality, comes from and is an integral aspect of the relationship
between the child and her parents. Fowler addressed the ways that
faith forms in early attachment relationships and helps us see "the
essential covenantal pattern of faith as relational" (p. 17). He explained:

> Our first experiences of faith and faithfulness begin with birth.
> We are received and welcomed with some degree of fidelity by
> those who care for us. By their consistency in providing for
> our needs, by their making a valued place for us in their lives,
> those who welcome us provide an initial experience of loyalty
> and dependability. And before we can use language, form
> concepts or even be said to be conscious, we begin to form our

first rudimentary intuitions of what the world is like, of how it regards us and of whether we can be "at home" here. (p. 16)

Thus, Fowler speaks here to how faith contributes to the child's sense of himself in the world. Further, Fowler argued that faith as imagination contributes to the child's experience and image of what the world is like. In his words, "Faith images a unifying grasp of the ultimate conditions of existence. Faith is imagination as it composes a felt image of an ultimate environment. We image from our experiences of relatedness in the covenantal contexts of our lives" (p. 33). As a contribution to the development of a sense of self, faith is a relational pattern constituting the child's view and experience of the world. From this view and experience, the child "makes sense" (p. 33) of his life, but this is not a static view or understanding of one's life; rather, faith is "dynamic and continually changing" (p. 33).

In addition to Fowler's (1981) contribution to this discussion, one chapter by Kneezel and Emmons (2006), in their paper in *The Handbook of Spiritual Development in Childhood and Adolescence* (Roehlkepartain et al., 2006a) also addressed this topic. Kneezel and Emmons's (2006) "Personality and Spiritual Development" was originally published while Kneezel was a graduate student working under the tutelage of Emmons, professor of psychology at University of California at Davis. Kneezel is primarily interested in religious motivation, whereas Emmons has focused on personality psychology, spirituality, and subjective well-being. He is currently editor in chief of *The Journal of Positive Psychology*.

Kneezel and Emmons (2006) argue that "religious experience in general has real, examinable effects on one's personality" (p. 266). Further, they state that "those aspects of personality most relevant to spiritual development constantly evolve to incorporate new life experience" (p. 266). They ground their argument in Self-determination theory, which is a motivation theory stating that "people strive toward structure and coherency between one's self and one's experiences" (p. 266).

Self-determination theory (SDT) proposes that there is an "organismic, core-self" (Kneezel & Emmons, 2006, p. 267) that "develops through a process of action that begins in infancy" (p. 267). This core-self is developed through an ongoing, autonomous process of integration and differentiation. Embedded within this process are the individual's basic needs of autonomy, relatedness, and competence. In terms of SDT and spiritual development, Kneezel and Emmons propose,

> A religious or spiritual outlook on life can provide one with an overarching theme or goal that helps to unify the person's self. A person also strives for relatedness and integration of the self with others. In addition to a sense of relatedness with parents and other loved ones, integration with others might also include unity with a higher being such as God (i.e., relatedness to God) or the sacred. (p. 268)

So not only does spirituality help "unify the person's self," according to the authors, but the need for relatedness within the autonomous process of self development also affords the opportunity to integrate with a higher being, the sacred, or possibly the (sacred) natural world.

## Review of the Literature on Self and Sense of Self Development

*Introduction.* One of the most fundamental spiritual, philosophical, and psychological questions asks who are we, as human beings. We seem to be in a perpetual state of asking this question and others, getting at the innermost experience of being human in relationship with others and the world around us. As Daniel Stern (1985) stated in the introduction to *The Interpersonal World of the Infant*, "the self and its boundaries are at the heart of philosophical speculation on human nature, and the sense of self and its counterpart, the sense of other, are universal phenomena" (p. 4).

Beginning with the giants of depth psychology such as James, Jung, and Freud, psychologists have continuously engaged with questions about the self. Is the self constructed, does it emerge, or is it to be discovered? Is there a true self? A false self? Is the self genetically determined, a spiritual endowment, or a product of upbringing? Is it contained within the individual or are the boundaries mingled with a collective self? Is the self a structure, a set of processes, an archetype, a complex, or a context-dependent relational experience? These are some of the questions addressed in the literature on the self and its development.

In addressing all of these questions and many others, the body of literature on self and sense of self development is vast. Therefore, this section of the review will give relevant samples primarily from developmental psychology, contemporary psychoanalytic psychology, and Jungian psychology. Literature from these three arenas was chosen based on how each illuminates different aspects of my topic, particularly with regard to children. In addition, in psychoanalytic investigations of the self and sense of self development there is a tradition, notably in Stern's (1985) seminal work, of integrating findings from empirical studies such as those typically conducted by developmentalists. Stern and other psychoanalytic authors integrate empirical data from infant observation with psychoanalytic inferences to penetrate intrapsychic developmental processes occurring beyond our ability to observe (Stern, 1985). Some Jungian psychologists have also integrated the findings of psychoanalysts and developmentalists with foundational Jungian concepts such as that of the archetypes (e.g. Jacoby, 2008; Fordham, 1994; Main, 2008; Sidoli, 1998). Along these lines but from a different perspective, depth psychological scholar Eva Simms (2008) made a unique contribution to the discussion of self, specifically regarding the question of interiority, with her reinterpretation of developmentalists' findings from a "nondualistic, existential perspective" (p. 3).

In the context of the current study I was particularly focused on the process and progression of the sense of self and curious about both conscious and unconscious contributions to this process. For this study, therefore, I investigated the literature with an eye trained toward understanding how both spirituality and the natural world might play a part in sense of self development. I examined the processes involved in development of a sense of self that might offer access to understanding the relationship between self, spirituality, and the natural world. Preceding an exploration of how sense of self develops, however, gaining a clear understanding of how scholars are conceptualizing "self" was extremely important.

**Conceptualizations of self are context-dependent.** When reviewing literature to examine conceptualizations of self, it became clear that a conceptualization of self depends on the purposes of the author and the context from within which the study was conducted (Brinthaupt & Lipka, 1992). Contemporary developmental scientists focus on changes throughout a lifetime (Lerner et al., 2010) and in particular, on self and identity as it progresses from infancy to old age (McAdams & Cox, 2010). Contemporary psychoanalytic self psychologists (e.g. Beebe & Lachmann, 2003) are interested in understanding the development and dynamics of the self in order to gain insight about pathology of the self and improve therapeutic outcomes for patients in psychotherapy. Jungian analytic psychologists also focus on therapeutic outcomes with particular emphasis on integrating conscious and unconscious processes. Each of these schools of thought conceptualizes the self and/or sense of self within a framework that supports the focus of their work. This section of the literature review will highlight salient points from these different conceptualizations in order for integrations, re-interpretations, and comparisons to take place in the study.

**Clarification of terms** *self, Self,* **and** *ego.* In order to include Jungian literature in this discussion, it is necessary to clarify different usages of terms such as *self* and *ego* in the selections of sample literature. Although there is more than simply a difference in terminology when it comes to comparing Jungian literature with psychoanalytic or developmental scientific literature, from my investigations it appears that some parallels may be drawn between formulations of *self* and *ego*. Where psycho-analysts and developmental psychologists use the term *self,* Jungian's would typically use the term *ego,* (especially when not writing from a developmental perspective) thus an adequate comparison may be made between these two terms. In contrast, *self* generally has a very different meaning in the Jungian literature (Stein, 1998, p. 151) than it does in both the psychoanalytic and developmental literature and does not find adequate parallel in these adjacent realms. In Jungian literature this term is frequently capitalized, which I will do from here forward when refer-ring to the Jungian *Self,* signifying a meaning greater than the individual self. Although even in the Jungian literature, as in the other broad realms of thought on the topic, not all conceptualizations of Self are exactly the same, the feature distinguishing the Jungian formulation of Self from the other bodies of work is the archetypal, collective dimension (Stein, 1998); this feature of the Self is not found in psychoanalytic or main-stream developmental literature.

**Self as both subject and object.** Discussion and exploration of the self is organized to a large extent around the idea that the self can take *itself* as the object of its own reflection (Harter, 1999). As in the literature review on spirituality in psychology, James's (1890) monumental work has had a profound influence on the scholarly discussion of the self in the developmental and depth psychological arenas. James (2008) put forth the idea of the dichotomous self, having both the *I* and the *Me* aspects to it: The I-self or knower is the part that can reflect on itself; the Me-self or known is the object of reflection. James's conceptualization of the dichotomous self is referred to repeatedly in the literature (e.g., Fonagy, Gergely, Jurist, & Target 2002; Fordham 2002; Harter, 1999; McAdams & Cox 2010) and evidently serves as a useful construct in the discussion.

Cognitive developmental scholar Susan Harter (1999) identified the self as a "cognitive construction" (p. 7) involving I-self, cognitive processes responsible for constructing the self-theory of the Me-self. This is echoed in developmental psychologists McAdams and Cox's (2010) work, who discuss the I-self as process and the Me-self as product. Psychoanalytic psychologists Fonagy et al. (2002) refer to the "agentive" and "representational" (p. 3) aspects of the self, corresponding to the I-self and the Me-self respectively. Somewhat differently applied but under the same Jamesian construct, Jungian analyst and developmental scholar Michael Fordham (2002) wrote about the I-self as "pure ego" (p. 97), connecting to a largely unconscious, archetype of the Self.

Although other authors reviewed for this study discuss the self-reflective nature of the self, they conceptualize it according to the focus of their examinations, which were not exclusively on the self, per se. For example, psychoanalytic self-psychologists Lichtenberg, Lachmann, and Fossage (2011) identify "recursive awareness" (p. 51) in the context of Lichtenberg's (2001) motivational systems theory. Rather than emphasizing recursive awareness (or conscious self awareness) as instrumental in self-development, he positions it as one of several foundational invariants upon which the motivational systems draw. Another example comes from Alan Sroufe and his colleagues, who identified the emergence of self-awareness as a key aspect of development during the toddler period (Sroufe, Egeland, Carlson, &

Collins, 2005). Simms (2008), in a hermeneutic phenomenological study of childhood, proposed a different perspective on this quality of self-reflective functioning; she asserted that the interiority of the self, required for self reflection, is an "illusion" coming from "an invisible symbolic activity" (p. 216) of the mind. Finally, renowned Jungian analyst Warren Colman (2008) makes a differentiation between *having* a self and *being* a self wherein self-reflective consciousness is necessary to know one *has* a self although not necessary to *be* a self. Although James's I-self/Me-self dichotomy serves as an organizing construct in the discussion of self, the essential feature of self-reflective awareness or the subject/object dichotomy thus is found throughout the literature, whether it is articulated under this Jamesian construct or a similar conceptualization.

**Theory of self from developmentalists.**

*The self as social and cognitive construction.* Harter (1999), a developmental psychologist and leader in her field on the topic of the self, offered a cognitive developmental perspective in her book, *The Construction of the Self.* This work examined the self as a social and cognitive construction with emphasis on the "*verbal* self-representations of self that begin to emerge toward the end of the second year of life" (p. 25). Language-based, memory-dependent, self-representations and social interactions are said to shape the self-structure of the child in early childhood. As additional developmental capacities come into play, self-representations continue to evolve throughout childhood and adolescence.

Drawing on Stern's (1985) groundbreaking work, *The Interpersonal World of the Infant,* to emphasize the significance of language in construction of the self, Harter (1999) cited Stern in asserting that when language emerges, the self acquires a powerful tool for use in its construction. She wrote, "With the emergence of language comes the ability to construct a narrative of one's 'life story' and therefore to develop a more enduring portrait of the self" (p. 32). Interestingly, Stern (1985) began *The Interpersonal World of the Infant* with a statement of his intention to study the *preverbal* infant's "non-self-reflective awareness" (p. 5). He clarified, "We are speaking at the level of direct experience, not concept" (p. 5). Whereas Harter (1999) uses Stern's (1985) work to support her emphasis on the cognitive-developmental aspect of self-development, Stern himself was particularly interested in the subjective experience of the preverbal infant. Harter's (1999) work, although thorough in its treatment of the cognitive and social aspects of self-development, does not consider spirituality or the natural world in the development of self or self-representation.

*Self as "actor, agent, and author."* Another developmental perspective, taken by authors McAdams and Cox (2010), comes from the same textbook as the Scarlett and Warren (2010) chapter on religious-spiritual development reviewed in the section on spiritual development. This text was chosen for its developmental theorizing on the self and because it offers an opportunity to see what contemporaries within the same field are saying about the topics addressed in this study. In their meta-analysis of studies on the topic, McAdams and Cox (2010) reviewed the historic lineage of ideas that shaped the "modern self" (p. 160). The *modern self* is defined as the reflexive self—the self that differentiates between inner and outer worlds, exercises executive control, and can take itself as an object of its own knowing. They then reviewed an interdisciplinary collection of literature on the self using the gross lens of life-span development. They refined the focus by applying James's I-self/Me-self dichotomy as a way to talk about the I-self as process that shapes the Me-self as product. Having identified these two points of focus, they then "sketch a new theoretical framework for conceptualizing the self" (p. 159) using McAdams's three-layered theory of personality. McAdams's theory "argues that people's internalized life stories are layered over their characteristic goals and values, which are in turn layered over their core dispositional traits" (p. 159). The theory demonstrates how these three layers of personality are interwoven with the I-self processes of social action, agency, and authorship.

McAdams and Cox's (2010) view, as representative of the life span developmental perspective, depicts an emphasis on I-self processes, or in other words, conscious processes that are closely related to what a Jungian developmentalist might call ego-development. The authors explained the thrust of their work in this chapter as being, "about how the three guises of human selfhood—actor, agent, and author—develop and interact with each other from infancy through old age" (p. 159). Although McAdams and Cox (2010) make reference to James's spiritual self—the chapter explores neither the nature of the spiritual self in depth nor how spirituality affects the development of a sense of self. and the authors do not explicitly investigate the question of how the natural world plays a part in the development of a sense of self. Their work, however, is most useful for the current study in its treatment of identity development and how the three guises of the self—actor, agent, and author capture the self's role in its own development.

*Dynamic systems: solutions seeking versus teleology.* McAdams and Cox's (2010) chapter serves as a good example of the trend in the literature toward theories that integrate multiple dimensions of ongoing interactions, based on dynamic systems theory. Rather than conceptualizing a linear progression of development, they identify as many of the multiple layers of interaction as possible and try to understand the complexity of interactions involved. In 1994, cognitive developmental scientists Thelen and Smith (1994) argued for a shift from the concept of "design" to the concept of "relation" in development (p. xix). The relation concept highlights interactions between many factors that together make up the developmental pathway of the organism. This is in contrast to former theories that would see development unfolding in a linear fashion according to an intrinsic design of some kind. They explained:

> The grand sweep of development seems neatly rule-driven. In detail, however, development is messy. As we turn up the magnification of our microscope, we see that our visions of linearity, uniformity, inevitable sequencing, and even irreversibility break down. What looks like a cohesive, orchestrated process from afar takes on the flavor of a more exploratory, opportunistic, syncretic, and function-driven process in its instantiation. (p. xvi)

With an eye toward understanding human behavior and cognition, Thelen and Smith proposed a model of development that sees the interplay between multiple elements coming together to "seek . . . solutions" (xix). What appears to be a "neatly rule-driven" (p. xvi) orchestration of elements following a grand, unifying design, is actually a process requiring the use of a different sensibility capable of appreciating something beyond the simplicity provided by the notion of a nice, neat design at work behind the scenes. Rather, they argue,

> There is complexity. There is a multiple, parallel, and continuously dynamic interplay of perception and action, and a system that, by its thermodynamic nature, seeks certain stable solutions. *These solutions emerge from relations, not from design* [emphasis added]. When the elements of such complex systems cooperate, they give rise to behavior with a unitary character, and thus to the illusion of structure. But the order is always executory, rather than rule-driven, allowing for the enormous sensitivity and flexibility of behavior to organize and regroup around task and context. (p. xix)

Although Thelen and Smith, to my knowledge, have not specifically addressed the question of self and sense of self development in their work, the theoretical model of development based on dynamic systems has made its way not only into the work of developmental psychologists but into the psychoanalytic literature as well. This is evidenced by reference to the theory in the work of Stolorow (1997), Beebe and Lachmann (2003), Lichtenberg et al. (2011), and others.

**Theory of self from the psychoanalytic literature.**

*Kohut and self psychology.* Coming from a traditional psychoanalytic background (i.e. post-Freudian), Heinz Kohut, father of Self Psychology, came to a different understanding of narcissism in his clinical work than that which had been generally understood in psychoanalysis (Siegel, 1996). He saw that narcissism has its own line of progression and is a normal part of healthy psychological development (Siegel, 1996). This understanding led to a new and broader concept of the self (Jacoby, 1990), a concept which places the self "as the center of the psychic universe" (p. 69). The self, as Kohut defined it, is a "nuclear self [with] a bipolar structure" (Kohut & Wolf, 1978, "Aetiology," para. 2). He also described it as the "core of our personality" ("The Emergence," para. 1). He explained:

> The *self*, the core of our personality, has various constituents which we acquire in the interplay with those persons in our

earliest childhood environment.... A firm self ... is made up of three major constituents: (1) one pole from which emanate the basic strivings for power and success; (2) another pole that harbours the basic idealized goals; and (3) an intermediate area of basic talents and skills that are activated by the tension-arc that establishes itself between ambitions and ideals. ("The Emergence," para. 1)

Under this "experiencenear" ("Closing," para. 6) formulation of the self, the infant is born with potential for a self but requires interaction with parents in order for the process of *"transmuting internalization"* ("Aetiology," para. 1) to take place thus allowing the nuclear self of the child to crystallize. The objects in an infant's world perform self-functions for the developing infant and are thus considered *selfobjects*. Through the process of interacting with selfobjects and the selective responses of the selfobjects, the bi-polar, nuclear self develops. The bipolarity of the self serves the continued development of the self beyond the initial emergence of the nuclear self. In *Disorders of the Self and Their Treatment*, Kohut and Wolf (1978), described the process as follows:

> The self arises thus as the result of the interplay between the new-born's innate equipment and the selective responses of the selfobjects through which certain potentialities are encouraged in their development while others remain unencouraged or are even actively discouraged. Out of this selective process there emerges, probably during the second year of life, a nuclear self, which, as stated earlier, is currently conceptualized as a bipolar structure; archaic nuclear ambitions form one pole, archaic nuclear ideals the other. The tension between these two poles enhances the development of the child's nuclear skills and talents—rudimentary skills and talents that will gradually develop into those that the adult employs in the service of the productivity and creativity of his mature self. ("Aetiology," para. 2)

In a 1991 article, relational psychologist Stephen Mitchell (1991) contrasted Kohut's view of the continuous, nuclear self with the view of the self as "multiplex and discontinuous" (Abstract). Rather than a unified, core self, similarly to Kohut, Mitchell elaborates on the view of the self as the result of relational interactions but, unlike Kohut, he sees these resulting in multiple selves that arise through multiple relational contexts. Psychoanalyst Philip Bromberg (1996) elaborated on this idea to talk about the dialectic between discontinuous states of consciousness or multiple selves and "the healthy illusion of unitary selfhood" (p. 3). He asserted that the dialectic process, rather than a unidirectional process, constitutes the growth of selfhood and self cohesion. As Bromberg conceptualized it, the psyche is responsible for "the maintenance of self cohesion" (p. 4). From Bromberg's point of view, psychological health entails "the ability to stand in the spaces between realities without losing any of them—the capacity to feel like one self while being many" (p. 4). Like Kohut, these authors theorized based on clinical experience with the focus on a better understanding of psychopathology, psychological health, and improved therapeutic outcomes.

Stolorow and Atwood (1994) discussed the "unconscious organizing power" of the "myth of the isolated individual mind" (para. 1). Building on the work of Kohut and proponents of self psychology, they challenged this prevailing myth with a perspective that emphasizes the "intersubjective foundations of psychological life" (para. 1). From this perspective, the self only develops within the intersubjective context, no matter the quality of that context. Rather than a reified self, these authors discuss the crystallization of self-experience. Thus the self from the intersubjective perspective is not a set structure but an organization of experiences, the organization of which occurs via the patterning of repeated experiences taking place within the intersubjective context.

*Senses of self.* Stern's (1985) seminal work involving infant research conducted in the mid-1980s, addressed the question of the self and the sense of self. He passed quickly over the question of the nature of the self, noting that the nature of the self "elude[s] the behavioral sciences" (p. 6) and moved on to investigate the *sense of self.* The sense of self, according to Stern, is not restricted to a conscious self awareness but rather begins preverbally, perhaps even in utero. He began *The Inter-*

*personal World of the Infant* with a statement of his intention to study the preverbal infant's "non-self-reflective awareness" (p. 5). He clarified, "We are speaking at the level of direct experience, not concept" (p. 5). In other words, what is the infant's experience of himself before he can even consider that he has a self or is a self? What is the nature of the infant's awareness before self-reflective awareness comes into play? These are the questions among others, addressed in his work.

Stern's (1985) interest in these questions about the infant's experience stemmed from developmental and clinical considerations. He specified,

> I am mostly concerned with those senses of the self that are essential to daily social interactions, not to encounters with the inanimate world. I will therefore focus on those senses of the self that if severely impaired would disrupt normal social functioning and likely lead to madness or great social deficit. (p. 5)

Stern argued that human beings have multiple senses of self, and that although they change over time, each becomes embedded within the new sense of self. He identified four senses of self: the emergent sense of self, the core sense of self, the subjective sense of self, and the verbal sense of self. In describing the sense of a core self, he stressed that this was "not a cognitive construct . . . [but] an experiential integration" (p. 30). To relate his work to the I-self/Me-self dichotomy then, Stern focused more closely on the pre-verbal I-self. However, this concept of the dichotomous self lends itself much more easily to a depiction of development beyond the emergence of the verbal sense of self when self-reflective awareness plays a greater role than it does to a depiction of the earlier senses of self. Theorists such as Lachmann (2004) building on Stern's findings have postulated a sexual sense of self which develops later.

Lichtenberg (Lichtenberg,1989; Lichtenberg et al., 2011) builds on both infant research and self-psychology to articulate a model of the self that is built through seven motivational systems. These motivational systems arise "solely from lived experience" (Lichtenberg, 1989, p. 2) and function for the fulfillment and regulation of basic needs. From his work with infant observation, Lichtenberg (1989)

concluded that "the self develops as an independent center for initiating, organizing, and integrating motivation" (p. 2). The *sense of self*
develops from *experiencing* the initiating, organizing, and integrating.
Affects experienced by the infant in interactions with caregivers signal
the fulfillment of basic needs. These are what Kohut and Lichtenberg
(1989) refer to as *selfobject experiences*.

   *Selfobject experiences.* Lichtenberg et al.'s (2011) motivational
systems theory addresses dynamic behavioral patterns that continue
to operate throughout life and are particularly relevant to therapeutic work and the therapist-patient relationship. Once again, the
selfobject experience facilitates the development of a cohesive sense
of self. When the self is cohesive it is free to meet its needs, not just
for survival but for those functions served by all of the motivational
systems (attachment, caregiving, sensual and sexual experiences, exploration, affilation, aversive response, and physiological regulation). The
"selfobject relationship refers to an intrapsychic experience and does
not describe the interpersonal relationship between the self and the
other objects" (Wolf, 1988, p. 184). The selfobject experience itself "is
thus not a reference to actual interpersonal relations or to the internalization of functions, but to an affect-laden, enhanced self-state"
(Lichtenberg, 2001, p. 134). This differentiation between the selfobject
and the selfobject experience is interesting for what it implies about
what other interactions or experiences might contribute to an *affect-
laden, enhanced self-state* (p. 134) and how these might affect the self
throughout life.

   Although Lichtenberg's (1989, 2001; Lichtenberg et al., 2011)
motivational systems theory addresses intrapsychic self processes,
there is also recognition of the intersubjective experience between
a parent and child or therapist and patient. Beebe and Lachman
(2003) also emphasize the intersubjective nature of interactions
between infant and caregiver or therapist and patient. They elaborated on a dyadic systems view of interactional patterns, building on
the increasing influence of the dynamic systems approach on developmental psychology as well as the increasingly relational emphasis
in psychoanalysis. The dyadic systems view states that intrapsychic
and relational processes are co-constructed, reciprocal, and interpenetrating. Beebe and Lachmann explained that dyadic processes,

involving both implicit and explicit modes of interaction, organize inner and relational processes. Implicit and explicit modes of interaction are akin to unconscious and conscious dynamics in the relationship. The authors indicated that both dyadic processes and selfobject experiences contribute to organization of the self, self regulation, and the development of trust and intimacy.

*Attachment.* Another perspective on the role of the relational context in development of the self comes from the literature on attachment. Neuroscientist and neuropsychoanalyst, Allan Shore (1994) addressed the question of the origins of the self within a psychoneurobiological model centered on "the principle of the development of self regulation" (p. xxxi). He later addressed the work of Kohut and self psychology, noting Kohut's "[ambivalence] about the incorporation of scientific data into the core of psychoanalysis and into the core of self psychology" (2002, para. 2) and focused on integrating the neurobiology of attachment with Kohutian conceptualizations of self development, lending scientific validation to Kohut's psychoanalytic theory of the self.

Furthering the study of the role of attachment on the self, is another major psychoanalytic contribution from Fonagy and colleagues. Fonagy et al. (2002) integrated Bowlby's scientific studies on attachment with object relations theory and proposed that attachment contributes to both affect regulation and mentalization which are in turn instrumental in self development. Mentalization, or reflective function, is said to be "a key determinant of self-organization and affect regulation" (p. 23). Beyond the primary adjustment of affect states, affects are said to "regulate the self" (p. 5) and mentalized affectivity is necessary in order for this to happen.

Building once again on Bowlby's attachment theory, Sroufe et al. (2005) made use of data gathered in the longitudinal Minnesota study they conducted to identify attachment as the "core" (p. 353) around which a "coherent emergence of self or personality" organizes. These authors were careful not to attribute functional outcomes directly to quality of early attachment but discussed it as primary in the complex, systemic development of the whole person. The quality of attachment lays the groundwork for future development and integration of experience within the child's self. Although other factors have great impact on the child's development, this primary bond between the infant and caregiver sets the tone for and attenuates all other orchestrations of the developing sense of self. The authors wrote,

> Attachment is critical and has a central place in the hierarchy of development because of its primacy. The infant–caregiver attachment relationship is the core, around which all other experience is structured, whatever impact it may have. Thus, we came to a position that early experience is never lost, however much transformation occurs in later development. (p. 353)

Sroufe et al. (2005) identified emotion regulation, arousal modulation, curiosity, social relatedness, and intimacy as "probabilistically" (p. 365) correlated with the primary attachment relationship. The self, in these functional outcomes, is therefore largely organized around the core of attachment. Although they were emphatic about the primacy of attachment Sroufe et al. were careful to position it "within a systemic, organismic view of development" (p. 365).

**Theory of self in the Jungian literature.**

*Introduction.* As in the psychoanalytic literature where integrations between developmental psychology and psychoanalysis occur frequently, the same may be said of Jungian literature. In her explication and chronicle of the developmental school in Jungian psychology, Jungian analyst and scholar Hester McFarland Solomon (2008) pointed out that while Jung was focusing primarily on the second half of life and the individuation process, the psychoanalytic world was advancing with the integration of mother-infant observations in psychoanalytic theory and clinical practice. Thus in the mid-1940s, Jungian-trained child psychiatrist Michael Fordham recognized the need to integrate Jungian concepts with findings from infant observation and psychoanalytic theory, becoming the founder of the developmental school of analytical psychology (Solomon, 2008). Further, a substantial body of literature addressing comparisons, integrations, and differentiations between Jungian theory and that of psychoanalytic theory exists, for example, in the work of Jungian scholars Mario Jacoby and Lionel Corbett. Corbett (1996) made use of Kohutian self psychological theory in his work on spirituality. Jacoby (1990, 2008) made conceptual comparisons between the work of Jung and Kohut as well as between Jung, Stern, and Lichtenberg, thus bringing Jungian concepts into dialog with findings from these psychoanalytic authors. For the purposes of the current study, a complete review of this body of literature making comparisons and integrations between Jungian and psychoanalytic concepts of self was not undertaken, due to the breadth of the territory it covers. Where relevant, however, reference is made to the findings from this work throughout the current study.

*The ego as part of the Self.* In order to bring the Jungian literature into a discussion of the self in the context of the sample literature reviewed above, it is necessary to focus here on Jungian conceptualizations of *ego* or *ego consciousness.* In *Aion* (1951/1969), an exploration of the phenomenology of the self, Jung gives a brief synopsis of his understanding of the ego as a point of entry into his discussion of the "supraordinate" (p. 3 [*CW* 9, para. 1]) concept of the Self. (Although Jung did not capitalize the term *self,* I do so in this study to make a clear differentiation between his use of the term and the use by other authors reviewed.) His definition of the ego was as follows:

> We understand the ego as the complex factor to which all conscious contents are related. It forms, as it were, the centre of the field of consciousness; and, in so far as this comprises the empirical personality, the ego is the subject of all personal acts of consciousness. The relation of a psychic content to the ego forms the criterion of its consciousness, for no content can be conscious unless it is represented to a subject. (p. 3 [*CW* 9, para. 1])

This definition might be somewhat misleading in that his use of the phrase "conscious contents" could lead one to believe that the ego is only about conscious processes or those processes of which a person is aware. He explains in *Aion,* however, that the ego has both psychic and somatic bases, and that each of these has both conscious and unconscious factors. Unconscious factors include the stratified layers of the unknown: that which may be brought into consciousness voluntarily via memory, that which may be brought into consciousness via psychological work but not voluntarily, and that which cannot be brought into consciousness at all (p. 4 [*CW* 9, para. 4]). He refers to the ego as the "point of reference" for the "field of consciousness" (p. 4 [*CW* 9, para. 4]) and asserts that what one knows about oneself, the conscious aspects of it, are only the "conscious personality" (p. 5 [*CW* 9, para. 7]).

To consider the "personality as a total phenomenon," wrote Jung (1951/1969, p. 5 [*CW* 9, para. 8]), one must take into account the ego's position as subordinate to the Self and "related to it like a part to the whole" (p. 5, [*CW* 9, para. 9]). The boundaries of the ego are defined by limitations to free will imposed on the one hand by the demands of the outside world and on the other by the "facts of the [S]elf" (p. 5, [*CW* 9, para. 9]) as they impose themselves on the inner, subjective world. Thus the dynamic between Self and ego is a major feature of the functioning of the ego in Jungian formulations.

*The archetypes.* The existence of the archetypes as "psychic universals" (Stein, 1998, p. 92), is one of the defining features of Jung's body of work (Hogenson, 2004). Jungian scholars such as Michael Vannoy Adams (2008) and Murray Stein (1998) point out that both Jung and Freud "acknowledged the existence of archetypes" (Adams, 2008, p. 107). Adams explains: "Philosophically, Freud and Jung were neo-Kantian structuralists who believed that hereditary categories of the psyche imaginatively inform human experience in typical or schematic ways" (p. 107). Through his exhaustive and lifelong study of myths, history, art, and literature, among other disciplines, Jung identified "parallels . . . found between images and myths of individuals and groups in unrelated historical periods and locations" (Stein, 1998, p. 92). Coming from the unconscious, the archetypes are the patterns or schemata that inform or guide human experience as well as the images and myths produced by individuals and groups. The experiences, images, and myths themselves are *archetypal* but are not actual archetypes. Jung (1947/1969) explained:

> The archetypal representations (images and ideas) mediated to us by the unconscious should not be confused with the archetype as such. They are very varied structures which all point back to one essentially "irrepresentable" basic form. The archetype as such is a psychoid factor . . . [and] does not

appear, in itself, to be capable of reaching consciousness. (p. 213 [*CW*, 8, para. 417)

Particularly relevant to the current study, the developmental school within post-Jungian analytical psychology has been influenced in the formation of its perspective on archetypes by the object relations school and the work of Klein, Winnecott, Bion and others. More recently, research and developments in the field of child development, including cognitive science and attachment theory, have also contributed to the developmental perspective. The work of Stern (1985) on the senses of self has also had significant influence on the Jungian developmental school. The definition of "archetype" and "archetypal" have been honed and refined through engagement with the Kleinian conceptualization of object relations within the infant. Fordham (1994) recognized that both Jung and Klein theorized innate organizing structures within the infant that became activated through early experiences. Fordham drew parallels between the concept of the archetype and the concept of part objects. The archetypal image was then comparable to whole objects and thus a later development within the infant. The work of Winnecott and Bion helped to bring to the fore the importance of the relationship between the infant and the mother or primary caregiver. The work of Stern (1985) helped the developmental school bring more sharply into focus the process by which the infant makes use of the archetypes and archetypal images to bring about the development of consciousness and the ego.

The archetypes and archetypal images are a part of the infant's cultural heritage and are seen in the contemporary field of the developmental school to have a genetic correlate. They are, "deep psychological structures…grounded in instinctual experiences represented mentally via archetypal images" (Solomon, 2008). Sidoli (1998) writes,

> The archetypes are conceived as organizers of experience and are activated by deintegrative-reintegrative sequences in the self. They form an ontological link within the human species, storing ontogenetic psychosomatic information that is expressed in each individual's idiosyncratic manner, offering the infant typical imagery in which to clothe his experience. (pp. 114-115)

An example of the constellation of an archetype within the infant is the Great Mother versus the *Devouring Mother*, which parallels *good breast/bad breast* conceptualization from the object relations school. Which pole of the archetype constellates depends upon the quality of the interactions between the infant and the caregiver.

Amongst the three major schools of contemporary Jungian scholarship—the classical school, the archetypal school, and the developmental school (Samuels, 1998) there is much discussion regarding the differentiation between the archetype *as such* and its archetypal representations (e.g., Hogenson, 2004). Although full treatment of this discussion is beyond the scope of the current study, the differentiation Jung makes between the archetype as such and its archetypal representations is significant when considering Jung's concept of the Self as an archetype of wholeness.

*The Self.* The Self, as Jung (1951/1969) wrote about it, "is a God image, or at least cannot be distinguished from one" (p. 22 [*CW* 9, para. 42]). Jung clarified in works such as *Psychology and Religion* (1938), that in discussing topics such as religion and God, he was not concerned with the ultimate truth or untruth of the existence of God or any of the claims made by religion. Rather, as an empirical, phenomenological psychologist, he considered these topics as suitable for psychological study because of their universality and the undeniably psychological aspect of them. Thus, while steering clear of the question of the actual existence of God from a theological standpoint, he addressed the psychological truth of the God image within the psyche. Jung (1951/1969) equated the God image or *imago Dei* with the Self. Stein (1998) explained:

> As Jung sees it, [symbols of the Self] are ubiquitous and authochthonic (that is, innate and spontaneous), and they are delivered to the psyche through the archetypal psychoid region from the archetype per se. The [S]elf, a transcendent nonpsychological entity, acts on the psychic system to produce symbols of wholeness. . . . Jung contends that every one of us bears the God-image—the stamp of the [S]elf—within ourselves. (pp. 158-159)

Symbols of the Self are symbols of "unity and totality" (Jung, 1951/1969, p. 31 [*CW* 9, para. 59]) that present themselves spontaneously (Stein, 1998). Equating these symbols with the imago Dei is based on the "objective value" placed on wholeness and unity (Jung, 1951/1969, p. 31, para. 60). Jung asserted that these symbols, often in the form of mandalas,

> occur not only in the dreams of modern people who have never heard of them, but are widely disseminated in the historical records of many peoples and many epochs. Their significance as *symbols of unity and totality* is amply confirmed by history as well as by empirical psychology. What at first looks like an abstract idea stands in reality for something that exists and can be experienced, that demonstrates its *a priori* presence spontaneously. Wholeness is thus an objective factor that confronts the subject independently of him. (p. 31 [*CW* 9, para. 59])

In Jungian formulation then, the Self is superordinate to the ego, is an archetype of wholeness as such, and is autonomous. Its function is, according to Stein (1998), primarily to keep the psychic system in balance and unified.

*The ego and its relation to the Self.* Whereas the developmental and psychoanalytic literature, as previously noted, has much discussion of the dynamics and consequences of interactions between the infant and other objects (in the psychoanalytic sense), the Jungian literature counterbalances this discussion with explorations of an intrapsychic dynamic between the ego and the Self. Corbett (1996) defines the relationship with his statement, "The Self is the archetypal underpinning of the self" (p. 40). Through his use of *self* and *Self* Corbett also calls to the fore the *likeness* between the two, as in the Biblical phrase, in the *image and likeness* of God (Genesis 1:26-27).

*The ego-Self axis.* Scholar and student of Jung, Erich Neumann (1954/1995) proposed an *ego-self axis* to describe the dynamic relationship between the ego and the Self. The relation between the ego and the Self is said to change over a lifetime wherein a trend, from ego-Self union, toward greater differentiation defines the first half of life and greater assimilation of the Self by the ego in the second half of life (Neumann, 1954/1995; Edinger, 1972; Stein, 1998). The first half of life is about development of the ego and persona, whereas the second half of life is concerned with the individuation process (Stein, 1998). Under Neumann's (1954/1995) construct of the ego-self axis, Edinger (1972) proposed a circular, alternating pattern of ego-Self separation and ego-Self union over the course of a lifetime.

*The primary self and deintegration-integration.* Fordham (1994) began formulating the notion of a primary self in infancy back in 1947. Through his work with infant observation and use of psychoanalytic (particularly Object Relations) and Jungian theory, in *Children as Individuals*, he proposed a "primary or original self" which is a "psychosomatic unity" (p. 75). Building on Jacobson's (1964) work, Fordham's concept of the primary self does not coincide with the Self as previously defined and it cannot be equated with the ego. The primary self or "original integrate . . . comprises the original psychosomatic unity of the infant, its unique identity" (Solomon, 2008, p. 140).

Through disruptions beginning with the psychosomatic trauma of birth and continuing throughout development, the self "deintegrates," according to Fordham (1994, p. 75), and then integrates once again. Rather than a continuously stable self, this conceptualization of the self has unstable states which are necessary for growth and development. Fordham explained that the deintegration (not to be confused with disintegration) and integration process is managed first solely by the self but soon thereafter by interaction between the ego and the self. The ego is itself a product of the deintegration process. During the deintegration-integration process "primitive modes of behavior and the existence of organised fantasies" (p. 74) are said to be organized by the archetypes.

**Theory of self according to Roberto Assagioli and psychosynthesis.** Roberto Assagioli, Italian psychologist and father of the "psychosynthesis" approach to psychotherapy, was a young contemporary of Freud and Jung. He was the first psychoanalytically trained psychologist in Italy (Sorensen & Birkholm, n.d.) but his work was little known until the fourth force psychologists made a place for themselves, beginning with the work of Maslow. Although Assagioli was not a "Jungian," he knew of Jung's work, corresponded with Jung during his lifetime, and built upon many of the foundational Jungian concepts of Self and the unconscious. Assagioli is reported to have stated the need for a counterpart to depth psychology in a spiritual or "height" (Miller, 1972, para. 3) psychology.

Assagioli's (1976) formulation of the personal self or ego was as the "personal center of awareness and will" or the "I" (para. 12). Like Jung, he identified this personal self or ego in relation to a higher or transpersonal Self. Whereas Jung discussed the archetypes as existing in an unconscious, psychoid region and having two poles, with one pole being on the level of instinct and the other being a spiritual pole and the archetype, Assagioli wrote about the depths of the collective unconscious and the heights of the spiritual unconscious, which he referred to as the "superconscious" (para. 1). Assagioli used his own egg diagram to depict the levels of consciousness, from the collective unconscious to the superconscious. This diagram also identified the relation between the personal self and the transpersonal Self within these levels of consciousness.

For Assagioli (1976), the superconscious is a nonpersonal level of psychic phenomena of the same general quality as the personal psyche but at a higher level. He then makes a differentiation, however, between the superconscious and the Self, with the superconscious being process-oriented and experiential while the Self exists as unchanging. Assagioli stated that the Self exists as a transcendent reality in and of itself, not as process but as an ontological reality beyond superconscious processes experienced by individuals. He clarified:

> The Self is like the pivot point, or hinge of a door; the door swings, but the hinge remains steady. Yet, the Self is not only the focal point around which the many superconscious processes occur; it is also the *cause* of those processes, and the source of the energy that makes them possible. So the Self is the unchanging, enduring reality; a stable center of life on its own level, which has functions but *is not a function*. (para. 5)

As support for the existence of this ontological reality, Assagioli (1959) cited the spiritual works of some of his contemporaries:

> There are various ways by means of which the reality of the Self can be ascertained. There have been many individuals who

have achieved, more or less temporarily, a conscious realization of the Self that for them has the same degree of certainty as is experienced by an explorer who has entered a previously unknown region. Such statements can be found in Bucke's *Cosmic Consciousness* (10), in Ouspensky's *Tertium Organum* (45), in Underhill's *Mysticism* (61), and in other books. The awareness of the Self can also be achieved through the use of certain psychological methods, among which are Jung's "process of individuation" (28), Desoille's "Réve éveillé" (12), the techniques of Raja Yoga (52), etc. ("The Higher Self," para. 2)

Assagioli (1959) also cited philosophers such as Kant who "make a clear distinction between the empirical ego and the noumenal or real Self" ("The Higher Self," para. 3). In differentiating between the personal self or ego and the transpersonal Self, he explained: "This Self is above, and unaffected by, the flow of the mind-stream or by bodily conditions; and the personal conscious self should be considered merely as its reflection, its 'projection in the field of the personality'" (para. 3). Whereas Jung, in his descriptions of the collective unconscious, made less distinction between a spiritual unconscious and the rest of the unconscious—placing more emphasis on the archetypes in his explanation of the spiritual, Assagioli thus clearly emphasized the "higher" unconscious or superconscious. In both cases, the relationship with the Self is of central importance throughout the course of an individual's life.

Assagioli (1959) provided a succinct list of the stages necessary in order for a person to "free himself from . . . enslavement and achieve an harmonious inner integration, true Self-realization and right relationships with others" ("The Collective Unconscious," para. 7). This list demonstrates the focus of his approach:

1.  Thorough knowledge of one's personality.
2.  Control of its various elements.
3.  Realization of one's true Self—the discovery or creation of a unifying center.
4.  Psychosynthesis: the formation or reconstruction of the personality around the new center. (para. 9)

Assagioli was therefore focused primarily on adult psycho-spiritual growth. Although he wrote about the use of psychosynthesis in education he did not spend a great deal of time discussing the development of the personal self or ego in the life of the infant and child.

**A theological perspective on the human being as "psychosomatic unity."** Given that the current study explores the interrelations between self, spirituality, and the natural world, it is worthwhile to very briefly note a relevant theological perspective which might have bearing on this question. Particularly with regard to the aspect of the question addressing the relationship with the natural world, consideration for any physical aspect of the self is important. In the Judeo-Christian theological context the question concerns the soul and the body— whether there is an immortal soul housed within the body. Clearly, no one unified perspective on this question exists, and the question itself has been the source of theological and philosophical debate for untold numbers of years; therefore, a concise statement addressing this issue may contribute to the current study. It appears to me to be directly relevant to an investigation of the relationship between the sense of self and spirituality.

Anderson (1999), professor emeritus at Princeton Theological Seminary and Old Testament scholar, addressed the question of body and soul in his book, *Contours of Old Testament Theology*. He stated,

> Human nature is not a dichotomy—a body of mortal flesh and a deathless soul, as in some philosophies, but rather a unity of body and spirit, an animated body—*terra animata* (animated soul), as Augustine put it. This view is expressed classically in the creation story found in Genesis 2, according to which the Lord God infused "spirit" (life force) into a lump of clay and it "became a living *nephesh*" (Gen. 2:7; NRSV: "a living being"). The Hebrew word should not be translated "soul," if that means an immortal essence, but rather "person" or "self." The self is a unity of body and spirit, a psychosomatic unity. That humans are "embodied beings," not a duality of body and soul, is shown by recent research in genetics. (p. 320)

This idea is echoed in the work of Colin Crowder (2000), professor of theology and religion at Durham University. Defining the term *humanity*, he stated,

> For many theological anthropologists, it is axiomatic that the original Christian vision of humanity followed the Jewish tradition in affirming human life as a "psychosomatic unity", distinguishing, but never separating the soul and the body as different dimensions of human existence. . . . The insistence that the human being is an "embodied soul" or an "ensouled body", and not a soul somehow occupying a body, is now not just the conclusion of arguments in theological anthropology but also the premiss of arguments in some other theological disciplines, and this is one measure of success of the campaign against dualism in the second half of the 20th century. (p. 313)

As noted earlier in this section of the review of the literature, definitions of self are context-dependent. This is also true in the above theological definition of the self as a psychosomatic unity. The theological context specifically addresses the spiritual nature of the self and identifies it with the body, rather than seeing the soul and body as separated. Although much in the psychological literature does address the self-body relationship, what this theological definition adds is the spiritual component. There is not a differentiation between the self and the spiritual, rather the self is spiritual and includes the body in its consitition. As biblical scholar Ludwig Kohler (1957) explained,

> *man is a living soul.* This sentence, which corresponds easily to Gen. 2:7, says three things: It says first of all that man became a living soul and now is a living soul. It does not say that man *has* a living soul. Soul is the nature of man, not his possession. . . . The second thing that the sentence says is that man is a soul. Were man only flesh made from the dust he would be only body. Were man only spirit without body, he would be formless. (p. 142)

## Review of the Literature on the Human-Nature Connection

**Clarification of the terms** *nature, the natural world,* **and** *the unnatural world.* For the purpose of the current study, the terms *nature* and *the natural world* are used interchangeably. When these terms are used, they refer to nature as a whole, excluding human beings and manufactured objects. Human beings are clearly part of the natural world in that we are a biological life form on the planet; a distinction is made, however, between human beings and the rest of the natural world in order to the examine the relationship between them. Spending time in the natural world therefore would generally mean being outside of man-made structures where nature, rather than manufactured objects or manmade structures, predominates. In urban settings, the natural world may, for the most part, be relegated to city parks but one would also typically find nature in the form trees and other plants, birds, rodents, domestic animals, the sky, the clouds, and the natural elements throughout the urban environment. Although people would have much more difficulty in urban settings finding areas where the natural world predominantly characterizes the setting, there are often areas where this would be the case within most major cities. There are also areas of urban settings where the natural world is almost completely absent, aside from access to the sky, possibly birds and rodents, and the weather. In circumstances where people have little to no access to the natural world due to the dominance of manmade objects and structures, this would be considered the "unnatural world."

**Introduction.** There is plenty of research on the human-nature connection showing the benefits of time spent in nature and there are many therapies based on this. There is animal assisted therapy, horticultural therapy, equine assisted therapy and place based therapy. The therapist is decentered in these forms of therapy and the natural world serves as medium of healing and transformation.

Contemporary authors of ecopsychology and ecotherapy take issue with the "use" of the natural world specifically as therapy for humans and see more of a reciprocal interaction between the human being and the natural world. A shift from the anthropocentric view of the natural world, to the biocentric view, is reflected in many areas of study, not just ecopsychology. For example, there is a whole new literary discipline called ecocriticism, which looks at literature from the perspective of the environment. Clearly, there is a major trend pushing for a shift in perspective on the human-nature relationship, which, in large part, disputes the Biblical notion of human dominion over the earth. The current study, however, has specifically to do with understanding how the human-nature relationship affects the sense of self in children. Is there a spiritual connection between children and the natural world or is spirituality itself embedded in the natural world? How exactly do we look at the relationships between the sense of self, spirituality and the natural world in children? The following review highlights some of the fundamental ideas in the literature on the human-nature connection and specifically the child-nature connection relevant to this study.

**Ecopsychology.** The field of *ecopsychology* offers us an important piece of this theoretical puzzle by looking specifically at the psychological relationship between human beings and nature. On their website, the International Community for Ecopsychology (2004) defines the relatively new field of ecopsychology as follows:

> Ecopsychology . . . is situated at the intersection of a number of fields of enquiry, including environmental philosophy, psychology, and ecology, but is not limited by any disciplinary boundaries. At its core, ecopsychology suggests that there is a synergistic relation between planetary and personal well being; that the needs of the one are relevant to the other. ("What is Ecopsychology," para. 1)

Considered one of the founders of ecopsychology (Coope, 2010), Theodore Roszak first came up with the term *ecopsychology* back in 1990 after participating in a "psychoecology" discussion group in Berkeley (Schroll, 2007, para. 3). On the website he edits for the Ecopsychology Institute, Roszak (1998) commented on the interconnectedness of the self and nature:

> If ecopsychology has anything to add to the Socratic-Freudian project of self-knowledge, it is to remind us of what our ancestors took to be common knowledge: there is more to know

about the self, or rather more self to know, than our personal history reveals. (para. 3)

He goes on to explain eight tenets of ecopsychology including the notion that nature and human beings are intimately connected, so much so that, "the core of the mind is the ecological unconscious" (para. 5).

In his seminal work, *The Voice of the Earth*, Roszak articulated (2001) his understanding of some of the problems of psychology and the influence of depth psychology's fathers, Freud and Jung. He critiqued the approaches of Freud and Jung and came to conclusions about their work with regard to its ecological mindedness or lack thereof. One of the conclusions he came to was that although Freud "could find nothing kindred or consoling in insensate nature, nature is still there in his work" (p. 64). Jung on the other hand, according to Roszak, "seems to abandon science" or in other words, his psychology is not grounded in "natural objects" (p. 64). Regarding Jung further, in his essay "Where Psyche Meets Gaia," Roszak (1995) asserted:

> in its most prominent interpretation, Jung's collective unconscious belongs wholly to the cultural realm; it is not filled with the tracks of beasts and the vegetative energies, but with high religious symbols and ethereal archetypes. It has more to do with Plato than with Darwin. (p. 12)

This appears to me to be a misinterpretation of Jung's perspective on the relation between the natural world and the collective unconscious. In an excerpt from "Archaic Man," Jung (2008) explained:

> Everything is alive [in the psyche], and our upper story, consciousness, is continually influenced by its living and active foundations. . . . The deeper we descend into the house the narrower the horizon becomes, and the more we find ourselves in the darkness, till finally we reach the naked bed-rock, and with it that prehistoric time when reindeer hunters fought for a bare and wretched existence against the elemental forces of wild nature. . . . Phylogenetically as well as ontologically, we

have grown up out of the dark confines of the earth; hence the factors that affected us most closely became archetypes, and it is these primordial images which influence us most directly, and therefore seem to be the most powerful. (p. 69)

Furthermore, Jung lamented the disconnection of human beings from the natural world, laying blame, in part, for this "dehumanization" at the foot of "scientific understanding" (p. 79) and the repudiation of nature worship by early Christians. He wrote,

> Man feels himself isolated in the cosmos. He is no longer involved in nature and has lost his emotional participation in natural events, which hitherto had a symbolic meaning for him. Thunder is no longer the voice of god, nor is lightning his avenging missile. No river contains a spirit, no tree means a man's life, no snake is the embodiment of wisdom, and no mountain still harbors a great demon. Neither do things speak to him nor can he speak to things like stones, springs, plants, and animals. He no longer has a bush-soul identifying him with a wild animal. His immediate communication with nature is gone forever, and the emotional energy it generated has sunk into the unconscious. (p. 80)

Therefore, although Roszak's work is important to the current study for what it brings to the discussion on the human-nature relationship, his interpretations of Jung's work do not do justice to some of the fundamental concepts in Jungian psychology. Both of these authors, however, provide a perspective on the human-nature relationship that counters the prevailing split between human beings and the natural world, demonstrating that not only are human beings physically dependent upon the environment for survival, we are also psychologically rooted in the natural world.

Eco-philosopher and spiritual activist Joanna Macy (2007) articulated a view of the human-nature connection wherein the boundaries around the individual self are not so clearly defined. "That is so" she wrote, "because as open, self-organizing systems, our very breathing, acting, and thinking arise in interaction with our shared world through the currents of matter, energy, and information that move through us and sustain us" (p. 153). Citing systems theory and the work of Gregory Bateson, she wrote about "the greening of the self" (p. 148), which involves "a wider construct of identity and self-interest" (p. 148). Rather than seeing ourselves as separate individuals serving our own self interests, she suggested a notion of self that includes the whole earth as our collective body. "The trees in the Amazon basin" she explained, "are our external lungs" (p. 157).

Will Adams (2005), author and professor of psychology at Duquesne University, explained the significance of the psychological connection with the natural world in his article, "Ecopsychology and Phenomenology":

> Ecopsychology involves a hermeneutic conversation between humankind and the other than human natural world. Through this dialogue we may realize that our ecological peril is largely a crisis of consciousness and culture. Therefore, this crisis cannot be resolved logically, with more or better information, or technologically with, say, better fuel sources or computers. Instead, it has to be resolved psychologically and sociologically via a transformation of consciousness and culture. (p. 270)

**Children and the natural world.** In his classic text, *Biophilia*, Edward O. Wilson (1984) articulated a view on the human-nature relationship that sees mental development as inextricably tied to the natural world. Human beings, he asserted, have an innate affinity for living organisms and the natural world because we are a part of the natural world. This innate affinity underlies the process of growth and development in significant ways, beginning in early childhood. The natural world provides "the matrix in which the human mind originated and is permanently rooted" (p. 139). He further stated that, "to explore and affiliate with life is a deep and complicated process in mental development" (p. 1). The essence of our humanity and existence, he argued, depends upon this affiliation. In his words: "To an extent still undervalued in philosophy and religion, our existence depends on this propensity, our spirit is woven from it" (p. 1).

Coming more specifically to the question of the child's relationship to the natural world, Richard Louv (2005), author of *Last Child in the Woods*, coined the term *nature-deficit-disorder* to bring attention to the harmful effects, specifically on children, of not spending time in nature or developing a connection with nature. Louv quotes Roszak on the lack of an acknowledgement of the connection between people and nature in the field of psychology:

> Psychotherapists have exhaustively analyzed every form of dysfunctional family and social relations, but "dysfunctional environmental relations" does not exist even as a concept. . . . The Diagnostic and Statistical Manual defines "separation anxiety disorder" as "excessive anxiety concerning separation from home and from those to whom the individual is attached." But no separation is more pervasive in the Age of Anxiety than our disconnection from the natural world. It's time . . . for an environmentally based definition of mental health. (Roszak, as cited in Louv, 2005, p. 44)

Social ecologist Stephen Kellert (2005), whose work also focuses on the human-nature connection, states that "the natural environment is profoundly related to people's physical, psychological and moral well-being" (p. 2). He notes also that there is a need for more academic investigation of this subject, in particular as it relates to the development of children. Although there has been some work in this area, the emphasis has been on "cultivating children's knowledge and appreciation of the natural environment, rather than the environment's role in their physical and mental development" (p. 64). His work outlines three areas of development that are affected by the relationship between the child and nature: cognitive development, affective or emotional development, and moral or evaluative development.

Cobb's (1977) book, *The Ecology of Imagination in Childhood*, addressed specifically the connection between children and the natural world and its impact not only on the development of the child but in shaping cultural evolution. Borrowing a phrase from Erik Erikson, she framed the work as an exploration of "the *genius of childhood* as a common human possession and a biological condition peculiar to man" (p. 15). This *genius* she described as "the spontaneous and innately creative imagination of childhood, both as a form of learning and as a function of the organizing powers of the perceiving nervous system" (p. 15).

Cobb (1977) did years of fieldwork observing children at play and also made use of the autobiographies of creative and influential adults to arrive at her conclusions. According to her close friend and the author of the book's introduction, Margaret Mead, she was also influenced in her work by her husband's hobby as a naturalist and the principles of evolution. This set a framework for the study of species in their environment. The question of context and the interactions between environment and organism therefore figured prominently into her explorations.

The child's sense of wonder and capacity for play lie at the root of the sensory/perceptual engagement with the natural world, according to Cobb (1977). This sense of wonder or "sense of the cosmic" (p. 28) she explained, is at the heart of the questions of both the child and the philosopher. These "cosmic questionings" (p. 28) are purposeful in the child's quest to "obtain, perceptually or verbally, some reflexive action from the external world to the self, in order to understand the world in terms of his own experience as well as through cultural explanations" (p. 28). The experiences most meaningful to the child in this sense are the sensory/perceptual experiences from engagement with the natural world involved in play. Cobb pointed out that the child's interaction with the natural world, like all organisms in their environment, is an "adaptive give and take" (p. 29) between the child and the environment, a form of play that informs the child's image of the world, which she referred to as "making worlds" (p. 51).

Although Cobb's (1977) work is useful to the current study for its emphasis on the role of the child's engagement with the natural world, the work has been criticized for its methodological shortcomings (Louv, 2005). There are, however, some useful connections to other work cited in this review, including her emphasis on wonder which was identified as one of the *spiritual* capacities of children (Hart, 2003), as well as the notion that the child develops a world view through engagement with the natural world.

## One final perspective on the human-nature connection: Ecotheology.

Ecotheologian and cultural historian Thomas Berry (2006) wrote about the human-nature relationship from the perspective of the earth itself as subject. He saw the earth as being in its own process of spiritual evolution, with human beings playing the part of conscious awareness. In Earth's evolution, the geosphere of inanimate substance was formed first, followed by the hydrosphere, the atmosphere, and the biosphere. The biosphere produces life on the planet which impacts the other spheres and each sphere ends up playing a part in earth functioning. The latest "power" (p. 19) to come along was the noosphere, which Berry referred to as the "mindsphere" (p. 19). This is the sphere created by human thought.

Rather than taking the perspective on human thought and cognition as being the penultimate achievement and "goal" of evolution, Berry (2006) saw this as another power of the earth's functioning, along with the former powers or "forces" (p. 19). From this perspective, human beings have a deeply reciprocal relationship with Earth. The evolutionary process of each affects the other. Berry's description of this in *The Dream of the Earth* demonstrates his sensitivity to the earth as a being in its own right. He explained:

> How great a marvel that these five forces in the light of the sun should bring forth the seas and the continents, the winds and the rain, and the profusion of blossoming flowers and other living forms that inhabit the earth. A magic world! Enchanting.
>
> But while we present these thoughts, we need to reflect especially on the mindsphere—the latest of these five powers that constitute the earth functioning. The landsphere and the other three powers that formerly functioned with such exuberant creativity seem now to have given over to the mindsphere the major share of directing the course of earth development. The earth that directed itself instinctively in its former phases seems now to be entering a phase of conscious decision through its human expression. This is the ultimate daring venture for the earth, this confiding destiny to human

decision, the bestowal upon the human community of the power of life and death over its basic life systems. (p. 19)

Although this statement seems to put responsibility for the entire planet's survival and evolution on human beings, Berry assures us that "the future shaping of the community depends on the entire earth in the unity of its organic functioning, on its geological and biological as well as its human members" (p. 23). Thus, the relationship between human beings and Earth from this perspective, repositions the earth as subject in relationship with human subjects. Our responsibility then becomes to understand ourselves within this relationship, rather than separate from the earth in our own functioning. In promoting a "cosmology of peace" (p. 216), Berry explained, "until the human is understood as a dimension of the earth, we have no secure basis for understanding any aspect of the human. We can understand the human only through the earth" (p. 219).

## Need for Further Research on the Topic

As the above literature review has shown, interest in children's spirituality has increased significantly, particularly Robert Coles's (1990) seminal work on the spiritual life of children. Whereas both religious and secular educators have been exploring spirituality and spiritual development in children for the past century, psychologists have entered the discussion much more recently. In particular, developmental psychologists have relatively recently undertaken an investigation of childhood religious and spiritual development. Clinical psychologists, on the other hand, and particularly depth-oriented clinical psychologists, have not focused on children's spirituality as a clinical issue. Further, Jungian analytical psychologists, particularly from the developmental school, tend not to isolate childhood spirituality as a topic of study but write rather from a perspective on the psyche as a whole that sees spirituality as integral to the process of development and individuation.

The review of literature on self and sense of self development, likewise reveals a vast and ever-growing body of literature from many different perspectives within the social sciences and the many branches of psychology. The review of literature particularly from developmental psychologists, psychoanalytic self psychologists, and Jungian analytical psychologists demonstrates that although the role of spirituality in self and sense of self development has not been a major focus for any of these disciplines, a rich discussion of the overlap between these two fields is ripe for the picking. Further, the explorations of implicit and explicit, verbal and nonverbal forms of intersubjective co-creation between caregiver and child or therapist and patient provide an enticing new vista inviting exploration of these dynamics and how they might be relevant in the relationship between children and the natural world. Further, how might the enhanced self-state provided by selfobject experiences be considered in the context of a relationship between the child and the natural world, as well as in the discussion of spirituality—for example, in experiences of transcendence? In Corbett's (1996) suggestion that the Self embodies in the child via mirroring of the Self by the child's selfobjects, there is an invitation to consider how this might be applied to the embodiment of Self via engagement with the natural world.

Although much research has been conducted in each of the fields of children's spirituality, self and sense of self development, and the human-nature relationship, this review of the literature reveals that the integration between these three areas has not yet been undertaken from a depth psychological perspective. A Jungian-oriented, depth psychological perspective in particular, seems to have much to contribute to the discussion on children's spirituality and likewise might have something to gain from the developmental perspective. With consideration for my own unconscious pull to this work, the potential areas of overlap between these three areas in addition to the noted absence of literature indicates a need for further research on this topic.

## Chapter Four

# Self and Sense of Self Development

During the preceding literature review, I positioned myself as a contemplative listener in the middle of the dialogue amongst the three bodies of literature reviewed. This contemplative place in the middle is a place where barriers and delineations, such as those made between academic disciplines or theoretical frameworks, give way in a dissolution process that renders each body more permeable and the dialogue more fluid. Rather than dissecting the dialogue, I listened for voices that issued from a place of truth and reality beyond the relatively superficial organizing strictures of academia. This was done with the notion that when one desires an intimate and penetrating knowledge of a tree, for example, one does not necessarily have to cut the tree down and count the rings in its trunk or take leaf specimens and look at them under a microscope in order to know something profound about the tree. There are other ways of knowing the tree which do not involve its destruction or degradation. These other ways of knowing do defy the rigid mandates of positivistic, empirical science, but as a theoretical study using a qualitative method, this study is unencumbered by the mandates of positivistic science and is in fact philosophically opposed to that methodology for this topic. I would argue that as a human being, I can directly know something vital and significant about a tree without relying upon those scientific mandates. Collectively, as participants in the "religion" of positivistic science, we seem to quite often give over our authority to the God of science, perhaps believing that science is all knowing. When we put all of our faith and belief in something outside of us, either in the tenets of religion or scientific fact, we surrender ourselves to false gods. As Jesus, Buddha, and other enlightened figures have taught, the way to the truth is through oneself and in oneself. This means that rather than now scientifically examining each aspect of the study and how it might be made to fit with other aspects of the study in a new configuration, the work of this study has been to listen more deeply, to hear "more truly" (Palmer, 1969) in order that in the following chapters the story of this study may be told more faithfully.

The main question being held at the center of this study asks how a child's developing sense of self is affected by both spirituality and the relationship between human beings and the natural world. In hindsight, it is clear that the question itself began from an analytical stance that supposes the child, the natural world, and spirituality can each be considered separately and, in fact, the literature review confirmed this supposition; there was ample literature addressing each individual aspect of this question. However, after beginning the review of literature, the clamor of voices within each body of literature threatened to obliterate the question itself even as the question attempted to draw in participation from all three realms. Only in letting go of the analytical stance that necessitates parsing into smaller and smaller segments did the dialogue become audible and coherent. Rather than an analytic stance, a contemplative stance that allows for things to come together in a more meaningful way clearly became necessary. In addition, I used a self-reflective process throughout the course of this study to further understand the relations and connections between between self, spirituality, and the natural world. It was from this stance that the voices in the literature have become more clear. These are voices speaking to the wholeness and integrity of human beings, rather than to the human being as specimen, or object, or inferior creature. My task in this chapter is to expand upon the findings that resulted from the process of reviewing the literature and thus reveal the origins of this notion of wholeness and integrity of human beings.

## Findings on Self and Sense of Self Development

Depth psychologists from both psychoanalytic and Jungian schools of thought have addressed the question of whether a self exists when human infants are born. This question is, of course, a demonstration of tolerance of the unknown because even though studies have been conducted to "prove" or "disprove" the existence of a self in new born babies, it is clearly impossible to know the answer to this with the kind of assumed certainty some have grown accustomed to expecting in psychological literature and elsewhere. Given the inevitable uncertainty of this starting point, psychologists have generally acknowledged that there is something there to begin with: a nuclear self (Kohut, 1978), an emergent sense of self (Stern, 1985), or perhaps a primary self (Fordham, 2002), and that the infant is "equipped from the beginning of life with rudimentary capacities for relatedness and access to his own inner state" (Lachmann, 2011, p. 59). Given this starting point, the dialogue then moves to an exploration of how the self or sense of self evolves.

As noted in the literature review, the perspective on how the self and sense of self evolves was informed by the authors' purposes of the explorations. In the current exploration, my purpose was in understanding the nature and function of the relationships between self, spirituality and the natural world in the child's developing sense of self. This purpose therefore serves as the particular filter through which I listened and contemplated what I heard in the dialogue.

**The infant-mother context and self development.**

> There is no such thing as an infant.
> Winnicott, 1987, p. 39

Perhaps the clearest statement arising in the dialogue about self and sense of self development is the importance of the *infant-mother context*. For the purpose of this study, the infant-mother context refers to the relationship between the infant and the primary caregiver, be it the biological mother, an adoptive mother, a biological or adoptive father, some other family member, or any other person responsible for primary care of the infant. Throughout the study, the term *infant-mother* is used for the sake of clarity and *mother* signifies any primary caregiver. Although there might actually be significant differences between the context cocreated between biological mother and infant versus other caregivers, it is beyond the scope of this study to explore these differences. The point of emphasis, therefore, is on the relational connection and context between infant and caregiver.

In the psychological literature there has generally been a progression over time from a perspective on the individual by him or herself to one encompassing greater and greater contexts of development, or as Stolorow and Atwood (1992) put it, "contexts of being" (p. 10). From depth psychology's beginnings, the relationship between the child and the mother has been recognized as having a great impact on the child's development and the subsequent psychological course of development for the person. What has changed over time is the perspective on what propels or moves the progression of the child's development, as well as how the relationship between infant or child and mother affects this development. Increasingly brought into consideration are the multidimensional aspects of this relationship such that it is now clear that mother and infant cocreate a relational *context* between them, not just a relationship.

The difference between a context and relationship, from my perspective, is the recognition and inclusion of the web of exchanges occurring in a context, as opposed to perhaps a more linear pattern of exchanges in what we think of as a relationship—linear because the pattern does not necessarily include the dynamic range of reciprocal interactions in the exchange, from physiological to psychological, explicit to implicit, and conscious to unconscious. In addition, a context takes into consideration the greater context in which the relationship takes place. Thus now it is clear that the interaction between the infant and mother provides a foundational, relational *context* for growth and development.

Three different aspects or directions for growth within this relational context occur. The first is relational growth between infant and mother. The second is the intrapsychic development of self and sense of self, and the final aspect is growth involved in the relation between the intrapsychic self and the transpersonal dimension or Self. None of these takes place on its own, without interacting with and being affected by the others. All three of these directions for growth take place within the "interactional matrix" (Lachmann, 2004, para. 6).

**Intersubjectivity, relational growth, and reciprocity.**

> The concept of an intersubjective system brings to focus both
> the individual's world of inner experience and its embedded-
> ness with other such worlds in a continual flow of reciprocal
> mutual influence. In this vision, the gap between the intrapsy-
> chic and interpersonal realms is closed, and, indeed, the old
> dichotomy between them is rendered obsolete.
> Stolorow & Atwood, 1992, p. 18

The shift in perspective from object-oriented relating to an intersubjective system brings into focus the subjective state of both mother
and infant in their interactions. The subjective state of both members
of this primary system is responsible for laying the groundwork for
interrelatedness between mother and infant, mother and child, and
child and others throughout life. In the formation, "crystallization"
(Kohut & Wolf, 1978, "The Emergence of a Psychology of the Self,"
para. 4), or growth of self, it is the "patterns of intersubjective transac-
tions . . . that unconsciously organize a child's subsequent experience
(Stolorow & Atwood, 1994, "The Ontogeny of Personal Experience,"
para. 2). According to Stolorow and Atwood (1994), these patterns are
stored in the prereflective unconscious of the child; however, the prereflective unconscious also exists in the mother as a result of the context
of her own early relationships and subsequent relational experiences.
To state the obvious, neither the child nor the mother is a blank slate.

The mother-infant dyad serves a regulating function (Stern,
1985) within the relational context. As the infant's subjective sense
of self emerges, as Stern (1985) recognized, the infant and mother
have the ability to share mental states. This occurs, however, outside of
awareness. Both mother and infant respond to one another's affective
state as part of a regulating process; but the regulation occurs both
*between* infant and mother as well as *within* each of them. As Beebe
and Lachmann (2003) stated, "each person must both coordinate
with the partner, and at the same time regulate inner state" (p. 1). This
emphasizes the reciprocal relationship between the infant and the
mother. Rather than there being a one-way transmission from mother
to infant, the relationship actually affects both individuals in the dyad.

"Each partner affects and is affected by the other, and within the dyadic interchange, each partner's self-regulation affects the interactive regulation, and vice-versa" (p. 4). Beyond this, the reciprocal exchange between the infant and mother is what constitutes both intrapsychic, self-regulatory functioning and interpersonal regulatory functioning. Thus this infant-mother context is critical for both intrapsychic and interpersonal growth of the self.

In addition to the coconstructed, regulatory processes that occur in the mother-infant dyad, there are both implicit and explicit exchanges (corresponding to nonverbal and verbal exchanges) that contribute to the growth of the infant's self. Much of the interaction taking place in the dyad happens implicitly, out of conscious awareness and even before conscious awareness is possible for the infant. Implicit exchanges occurring outside of conscious awareness include tone of voice, facial expression, and various other exchanges that inform the interaction without being explicit—such as a verbalization or even an explicit response to cries for hunger, discomfort, or sleepiness (Beebe & Lachmann, 2003). This means there is a whole host of influences affecting both infant and mother that give much greater depth to their exchange and which are likely never fully known. The effects of the implicit exchanges register not only psychologically but also physically in both affective state and proprioceptively (Lachmann, 2004). For example, the infant matches the mother's facial expression and "learns" in the body, how to make her own face do what she sees her mother doing by feeling it in her own face, which is known as "cross-modal matching" (para. 25). A very young baby "smiling" in response to mother is a simple example of this. Later, a baby clearly learns to smile responsively well before she is consciously aware of what she is doing; however, some of the implicit exchanges and cross-modal matching that occur are not even in the form of responsiveness but happen as part of the process of reciprocal attunement between infant and mother. This is more like string resonance between two stringed instruments; when a musical note is played on one of them, sound frequencies can cause resonance in the other, which means even though the note has not been played on the second instrument, the resonant string will vibrate as if they are singing together. By analogy, the cross-modal matching between the infant and mother seems to happen according to a kind of complex resonance between them. This highlights how much of the exchange within the infant-mother context involves processes occurring outside of conscious awareness. In addition, it emphasizes how the relational matrix entails affective or psychological exchanges as well as physiological exchanges.

Kohut and Wolf (1978) made the point in self psychological theory, that part of the responsiveness of the adult to the child depends upon the adult's imagination about the child in the form of "hopes, dreams and expectations concerning the future child ("Aetiology of Self Pathology," para. 2). In that the mother does not know that she is helping to shape the self of the infant through her own hopes, dreams, and expectations but simply has these for and about her infant, this type of contribution to the development of the infant's self can be said to be implicit in their interactions. A typical mother is not thinking about how her imaginations about the child will shape the child nor is she using this knowledge to shape her interactions or guide her behaviors, but it is happening nonetheless. Therefore, behind the behaviors or patterns of implicit interaction are the conscious and unconscious contents of the mother's psyche.

**Intrapsychic growth and subjectivity.** Within the intersubjective context co-created by the mother and infant, the infant also grows intrapsychically, laying a foundation for continued intrapsychic growth during childhood and beyond. As the infant engages in the relational context with mother, repeated affective experiences become organized intrapsychically as the sense of self emerges. The intrapsychic organization of experiences is necessary for growth of the self. In this sense, the self is a fluid pattern or organization continually integrating sensory, affective, and cognitive experiences. The pattern is fluid and subject to growth and change through repeated experiences of the same or a similar nature, as well as significant relational "events" and also traumatic events in the course of the infant and child's development. The fluidity of the pattern in the organization of the self is like a system of creeks and rivers, subject to naturally occurring ecological events (such as changes in weather and rainfall) resulting in a whole range of effects upon the course of the creeks and rivers while the overall pattern of the system remains relatively stable. This is in contrast to the idea that the self is a "structure" which connotes a more fixed, solid organization—man-made in fact, as opposed to a naturally occurring system with organization, yes, but still much more fluid than a "built" structure. Kohut's use of the term *crystallization* to describe what happens in the growth of the self is useful in the sense that crystals have a natural growth pattern (they are not *built* per se) but from my perspective this term leans toward a rather rigid connotation of "self" when discussed as an organization within the psyche. Nevertheless, a central aspect of the child's development of a sense of self is this intrapsychic organization beginning in infancy.

Stern's (1985) work has been useful to this discussion for many reasons but for my purposes at this point, his work is useful for calling to the fore the difference between the self and the sense of self. When "the self" is discussed, this is looking at the self as an object—I take my *self* as the object of my reflections or I look at the self in someone else—infants, children, mothers, others, etcetera, from the point of view of someone looking on. With self-reflective awareness—we have the capacity to do this even with ourselves, but the "sense of self" comes more from the subjective perspective of one's experience of oneself. This does not have to be a completely cognitive experience, in fact, Stern's (1985) goal was to investigate pre-cognitive stages in the infant's development. The "sense of self" depends upon the self—the self underlies the *sense* of it, but the "sense" of self is an ongoing activity or experience. It is never completely still or finished. Once again, this is a contrast to the self as organization or structure. The *sense* of self would be the *experience* of the fluid pattern of experiences described earlier.

From the very beginning of an infant's life, the sense of self entails a pattern of bodily experiences and what Stern (1985) calls the "memory" (p. 91) of these bodily experiences. Clearly, this is not memory in the cognitive sense, such that it can be called into awareness, but it is a bodily memory—sensory, muscle memory. The "emergent" (p. 46) sense of self Stern described is a sense of the organizing of these experiences beginning to come together. As Stern stated,

> the sense of an emergent self thus concerns the process and product of forming organization. It concerns the learning about the relations between the infant's sensory experiences.

. . . Product is the organization, or "yoking" of experiences.
Process is the experiencing of the organization, the experience
of organization-coming-into-being. (p. 46)

This organization is then used as a "reference point" (p. 46) for
continued sensing and organization as additional senses of self evolve.

The "core" sense of self, as Stern (1985) described it, then uses the
"reference organization" (p. 46) of the emergent sense of self in organizing experiences concerning the body—"its coherence, its actions, its
inner feeling states" (p. 46). The core sense of self does not supersede
the emergent sense of self, rather it comes into being as a continuation
of the organizing process of the emergent sense of self and exists as
an additional sense of self, similar perhaps to another form of sensory
perception. If the emergent sense of self is like the sense of touch,
then the core sense of self might be like the hearing sense. Both senses
(as well as the others) continue to be used throughout life and there
is an intersensory integration process going on behind the scenes all
the time and from very early in life (p. 286). The core sense of self as
described by Stern is primarily a bodily sense of self—a sense of self
that comes from the feeling of the organization and integration of
bodily experiences, including "inner feeling states" (p. 46). Once again,
the context cannot be separated from the bodily experiences; however,
the focus at this point is on the intrapsychic phenomena that consti-
tute the development of a sense of self. The sense of a core self has its
own relatedness but the relatedness occurs within the infant—relatedness of experiences, rather than interpersonal relatedness. This is what
Stern refers to as "core-relatedness" (p. 27).

Once the organization of a core sense of self is in process, this
serves once again as a reference point for another, very significant
sense of self to emerge. This is the "subjective" sense of self, which
Stern (1985) says emerges typically around the age of 9 to 18 months
old (p. 124). The subjective sense of self comes about as a by-product of
the infant's experience that mother or primary caretaker has her own
inner state that can be shared (or not) with the infant. Stern described
this as an experiential sense rather than a verbally rendered conscious
recognition. He wrote about this based on his observation of a new
kind of presence in the infant at this point. From this he inferred that

the infant now has this new sense of the other and with that, a new sense of her own subjective self. Experiencing relatedness with others both depends upon and simultaneously cultivates the subjective sense of self and "intersubjective-relatedness" (p. 27). This is not a language-based cognitive experience but a *sense* within the infant. Stern made this point clear:

> The domain of intersubjective relatedness, like that of core-re-latedness, goes on outside of awareness and without being rendered verbally. In fact, the experience of intersubjective relatedness, like that of core-relatedness, can only be alluded to; it cannot really be described. (p. 27)

After these first three senses of self have emerged and the infant's continued experiences have established their fluid patterns of organization, then the verbal sense of self begins to emerge. Language clearly will already have been a part of the infant's sensory experience in that she will have heard language being spoken, she will have experienced the vibration of the voice in the language being spoken, she will have experienced affect in connection with language and she will have experienced the implicit communications in the language well before she will be ready to process and understand the language itself. The senses of emergent, core, and subjective self, as well as these other modalities of experiencing language serve as the underpinnings enabling the sense of the verbal self to emerge.

Bringing in the Jungian perspective, the archetypes also contribute to the infant-mother context, working unconsciously to guide the patterning of experience within the infant's self organization. As understood in the developmental school, the archetype is an "emergent structure" without specific content of its own. There is no preformed image residing with the psyche of the infant but rather a potential for the archetypal image to become integrated into the psyche of the infant. In this way, archetypal images are products of early development and come about only after the infant has had many experiences, both internal and with the external world. Like the findings on attachment, though not directly causal to specific functional outcomes, the archetypes play a significant role in the developing self of the infant and child. This is particularly important in the consideration of the interplay between self, spirituality, and the natural world given that archetypes are bipolar, psychoid potentialities that tend to constellate toward one pole or the other, depending on the experiences and idiosyncrasies of the individual. Again as a parallel to attachment, when the quality of interactions between the infant and mother is "good enough" the positive pole of the mother archetype is more likely to constellate, manifesting in a generally positive relational pattern between mother and infant, as well as positive unconscious expectation on the part of the child as to other maternal figures, including perhaps, the natural world and the divine or Self.

**Selfobject needs and selfobject experiences.** An important aspect of the development of a *cohesive* self organization occurs through the meeting of selfobject needs and selfobject experiences. In the early stages of self development, a cohesive organization is more likely to occur when developmental "narcissistic" self-needs are met by the primary caretaker. This means, according to Kohut, that an aspect of normal self development is the fulfillment of needs for mirroring, twinship, and idealization (Siegel, 1996). The fulfillment of these needs allows the infant (and later the child) to internalize the experiences of having these needs met in order to develop a healthy sense of self-worth, assertiveness, strong ideals and values, and a sense of belongingness and connectedness to others (Banai, Mikuliner, & Shaver, 2005). Mother or primary caretaker is the "object" with whom the infant relates in order that the self can begin to organize—she is the object of the self; but the term *selfobject* does not actually refer to the interpersonal relationship. Wolf (1988) defined the selfobject as an "intrapsychic experience" (p. 53) within the infant; however, the fulfillment of the selfobject need—in other words, the selfobject *experience*—is what is responsible for the infant and child's "affect-laden, enhanced self state" (Lichtenberg, 2001, p. 134 ). It is this experiential *state*, when repeated often enough in fulfillment of developmental needs, that contributes to a cohesive self organization.

Lachmann (2004) also discussed an important feature of a cohesive self which is the capacity to experience "oneness mergerlike states and a bounded sense of self" (para. 17). In order for a calm, safe, and secure sense of self to develop, said Lachmann, the person must have the flexibility of self to experience both states: a sense of self, and a sense of oneness where boundaries are "yielded up" (para. 17). Lachmann and Beebe (1989) focused particularly on interactions between the infant and mother involving matching states, disruptions and repair as instrumental in the development of this capacity. Over time, this capacity continues to be cultivated throughout the child's development and into adulthood primarily through relational experiences.

**The self-Self relational context.** The final direction of growth occurring in the infant-mother context involves the inner relation between the self and the transpersonal Self. Within the context of the intersubjective, infant-mother dyad, the "ontological reality" of the transpersonal Self exists in relation to both subjects—infant and mother. Typically we discuss the infant's developing self or sense of self but put less emphasis on the mother's developing self in that discussion. Through their interactions, both mother and infant engage the transpersonal Self as selfobject. The relationship between them enables this engagement. Corbett (1996) discussed this in the context of the psychotherapeutic relationship but it applies equally well to the mother-infant/mother-child dyad:

> As is the case in any important life situation, there is also a *transpersonal or archetypal level* [emphasis added] of the relationship. . . . The archetypal level provides the spiritual underpinning of, and adds numinosity to, relationships in general. . . . The Self is of course unitary; unlike the personal self it has no boundaries, so that therapist and patient are immersed in the intersubjective psychic field which it produces. . . . It is insufficient to attribute the nature of the field that dominates the therapeutic relationship solely to the developmental histories of the two participants; as well, a supraordinate archetypal constellation affects both of them. (pp. 24-25)

As discussed, for the child, sense of self continually emerges over time. Stern described four senses of self and Lachmann (2004, para. 19) added another—the sexual sense of self; it may be that senses of self continue to develop throughout a person's life. The important point in this discussion, however, is that throughout this ongoing emergence of sense of self, an unconscious connection to the transpersonal Self underlies all of the processes discussed regarding both intersubjective and intrapsychic growth. The personal self is embedded within the transpersonal Self. As Assagioli (1959) articulated it, the personal self is a "projection" ("The Higher Self," para. 3) of the transpersonal self, or as Corbett (1996) put it, "the Self acts as a template or blueprint for the development of the subjective experience of being or possessing a personal self" (p. 40). Furthermore, he said, "The self correspond[s] to an inner predisposition determined by the Self" (p. 40). Thus selfobject needs are not only developmental, narcissistic self needs or motivational needs but are also Selfobject needs. In other words, they are shaped in part by the "archetypal underpinnings" (p. 40) within which the personal self emerges. In this way, when selfobject needs are met, the Self incarnates or becomes embodied in the personal self. Corbett explained:

> The embodiment of the Self occurs by means of affective experience, and the manner in which the developing child's human milieu responds to his affective states has a determining influence on the coherence and cohesiveness of the resulting personal self. (p. 40)

Another way of discussing the connection between the personal self and the transpersonal Self is by using Neumann's (1954/1995) articulation of the ego-self axis, which I will call the *self-Self* axis. There is an ongoing axis or connection between the personal self and the transpersonal self that exists throughout a person's lifetime, (although this connection may be damaged or severed.) The connection itself allows for a similar type of resonance as described between mother and infant to occur between self and Self, but the resonance occurs relationally and experientially within the context of the infant-mother dyad and other selfobject relationships. For example, the selfobject need, as defined by Kohut, for the idealizing parent imago, seen in the context of the self-Self axis, is a need for relation to the Self; in attempting to satisfy this need, the child projects the Self onto the parent as the idealizing parent imago (Corbett, 1996, p. 150). Intrapsychically this serves both to provide a more cohesive personal self organization and to integrate the transpersonal Self into the personal self organization. In Corbett's (1996) words:

> If the parent is able to carry these idealized projections, the idealized selfobject is gradually internalized, allowing self structures to be built which are an internal source of self-soothing, values and the numinosum, without fragmenting. The selfobject function thereby becomes an internal capacity to experience spirit. (p. 150)

### Conclusions on Self and Sense of Self Development

Although, clearly, the child's sense of self continues to develop in the context of relationships and integrates intrapsychic, interpersonal, and transpersonal experiences, the primary infant-caregiver relationship is fundamental to this ongoing development. As Sroufe et al. (2005) made clear, the early attachment pattern, although not *directly* causal to later developmental outcomes, is nonetheless of primary significance; therefore, the early infant-caregiver relational context is of primary significance to the child's development of a sense of self. It is within this context that the "nodes" (Lachmann & Beebe, 1989, p.142) are primed for integrating within the sense of self both spirituality and a sense of relatedness with the natural world. Lachmann (2004) identified the sexual sense of self as emerging beyond the verbal sense of self, as decribed by Stern (1985). I would argue that both a spiritual sense of self and a sense of self in relationship with the natural world are also possible later emergences within the child.

Beyond the observed interactions between the infant and the mother wherein one might witness the effects of responsiveness or lack thereof, as well as the idealizing, mirroring, and twinship or lack thereof, and the effects of secure attachment versus anxious or avoidant patterns of attachment, there exists a web of exchanges in this context that also have great impact on the child's developing sense of self. These are implicit, affective, and unconscious exchanges between the infant and the adult. In addition, all of this occurs embedded within a transpersonal context that is, by necessity, unconscious.

*Chapter Five*

# Children's Spirituality and Spiritual Development

In listening for the voices in the literature on children's spirituality and spiritual development, it once again became clear how difficult it is to isolate spirituality for discussion and separate it from the overall psyche. In order to integrate the findings from the review of literature on children's spirituality with the other aspects of the topic, however, I attempt in this chapter to highlight the most prominent points of discussion relevant to the research question.

Literature on the topic of children's spirituality generally addresses questions on the nature of spirituality and what role it plays in the child's development. Often the impetus for addressing these questions is a statement on the lack of recognition in the social sciences and education of the significance of the spiritual life of the child. This seems to stem from the fact that the spiritual life of the child was thought to be addressed in the context of religion thereby precluding a need to address it in the context of education or psychology. In this country, with its emphasis on religious freedom, clearly, the spiritual life of the child could not be addressed in the classroom when religion and spirituality were inextricably linked. In addition, in the field of psychology, discussions of spirituality had been marginalized due to an over-reliance on positivistic science and Freud's early dismissal of religious belief for its purported neurotic basis. Now that institutionalized religion plays less of a role in societal functioning than it once did, meaning that spirituality is not strictly relegated to the practice of religion, the recognition of the spiritual nature of the child has made its way into the field of psychology. In education, with more of a differentiation between religion and spirituality, the spiritual life of the child has begun to make its way into the discussion, at least in academia if not as much amongst policy makers. It is clear that spirituality may now be discussed outside the context of religion and that it is not inextricably linked with religion like it once was. This does not mean that religious participation is irrelevant to spirituality but that it is not a necessity for spiritual living and may, in some cases, be a hindrance to spiritual development.

Many authors in developmental psychology now advocate an acknowledgement of the importance of the spiritual life of the child to overall development. This is done through declarations such as Myer's (1997) statement that "Spirit is that property of being fully and wholly human" (p. 62) or Johnson's (2008) statement that "spiritual development is about orienting life toward what most vitally matters" (p. 26). Hay and Nye (2006) also argued that "children's spirituality is rooted in a universal human awareness; that it is 'really there' and not just a culturally constructed illusion" (p. 18).

Coming from the depth psychological perspective, Jung's overall orientation to psychology is said to have been a "psychology of the spirit" (De Laszlo, 1990, p. xviii). This is in itself a statement of the importance of the spiritual to overall development of the person in that his entire body of work was infused with recognition of the integration of the spiritual in psychology. Whereas Jung emphasized the individuation process as a spiritual growth process taking place in the second half of life, authors building on his work recognized the importance of the ego-Self axis from the earliest stages of life. The ego-Self axis is the connecting link between the individual self and the transpersonal Self functioning both as a capacity and an innate connection. Hence from a Jungian-oriented perspective, the spiritual has always held a place of prominence in a person's psychological life.

## Spirituality as That Which Makes Us Most "Human"

The field of psychology has always been interested in what differentiates human beings from our biological relatives in the animal kingdom. On the spectrum from the most "basic," animal-like nature of human beings to the most "evolved," distinctly *human* nature of human beings, *logos* or the reasoning mind has typically been considered the height of what makes us human rather than animal (Hergenhahn, 2005, p. 47). (The words *basic* and *evolved* are set off in quotes because these terms connote a value system which must be reconsidered in the context of this study.) Going all the way back to Aristotle, the human ability to think and reason has been regarded as that which differentiates human beings from all other life forms (Hergenhahn, 2005). In the literature on children's spirituality, however, that which makes us most human extends beyond the limitations of the reasoning mind to the spiritual. With the spiritual on one end of the spectrum, the other end would be the instinctual— that which enables us to meet our basic human needs for survival and comfort. The spiritual is therefore that which differentiates us from the other animals with whom we share so much, not the least of which is our living environment or the natural world.

When capacities such as wonder and wondering (Hart, 2003), are utilized in the direction of "Ultimate Unity" (Hyde, 2008, p. 43 ), they can be considered spiritual capacities. When they are utilized in the direction of meeting basic needs for survival and comfort, they remain the same capacities but they are being used in the service of more instinct-based endeavors. For example, much of the scientific, rational minded explorations of the world around us have to do with finding better ways to solve the problems of being physically vulnerable human beings subject to the elements, disease, the challenges of feeding, clothing, and sheltering, as well as the social structuring that best allows for these to happen. Many of the solutions to these problems likely started as open-ended ponderings or wondering about something unknown. Other capacities of the mind then play a part in shifting the quality of these explorations from spiritual in nature to what we think of a scientific or rational.

Although these two directions are generally considered to be opposing one another, it is not uncommon for the scientific to become spiritual when investigations reach toward ultimate answers. We consider the same capacities to be spiritual when they are cultivated and used in the other direction, toward making meaning, having a sense of purpose, having a sense of belonging and seeing a way to make a contribution to the whole. These capacities also serve to connect oneself to one's divine, sacred, or transpersonal source in answer to the age-old questions: Where do we come from and why are we here?

Spirituality is the capacity within human beings that allows for all of the states and activities of the human mind in its exploration of what it means to be human-not just the question of what it means to be human, but the experience of what it means to be human. Being in a state of wonder, wondering about something, relating to others, seeing the invisible (Hart, 2003) are all a part of the exploration of the experience of being human. Sensing awareness, mystery, or spiritual questing (Hay & Nye, 2006) are also part of this exploration. Self-reflective consciousness undergirds all of these activities.

The experience of transcendence is also undergirded by self-reflective consciousness and has to do with transcending or overcoming "each and every condition of our existence" (Myers, 1997, p. 62). It is the experience of submitting the self to something greater than the self or having a sense of connection with something greater than oneself. The experience of transcendence might also be expressed as a spiritual capacity—akin to what Lachmann (2004) discussed in his paper on the capacity for a sense of boundedness in conjunction with the capacity for merger or unity. The experience of transcendence involves a level of basic trust, which, in the context of spirituality, is faith.

### Spirituality as Reparation of Separation and Division

Typically, human beings experience multiple levels of separation and division that prove troublesome in some aspect of life. We sometimes have the experience of separation from God, separation from one another, separation from the natural world, or even separation from oneself. These separations and divisions mean seeing ourselves as "separate" and therefore in competition with one another, as more or less deserving than one another, or somehow more or less valuable than one another. Spirituality repairs separations and divisions in the quest toward "Ultimate Unity" (Hyde, 2008, p. 43). When we repair this kind of separation, we see one another as equals, we have greater tolerance for perceived differences, and we are more likely to be able to follow the spiritual maxim and ethical code to do unto others as you would have them do to you.

## Spirituality in Children

This simplifies the question of the nature of spirituality in children. Those properties, capacities, faculties, or sensitivities having to do with human consciousness and the self-reflective nature of our consciousness define the spiritual nature of human existence. In children, spirituality includes the capacities for wonder, wisdom, wondering, relating, and sometimes seeing the invisible (Hart, 2003). It also includes special kinds of "sensing" which we do not consider other animals to have, such as awareness sensing, mystery sensing, and spiritual questing (Hay & Nye, 2006). It includes the faculties of faith and morality, as well as gratitude and compassion. These all define the ineffable essence of what it means to be human and is the same for children as is it is with adults.

**Importance of the recognition of the spirit of the child.** In children, spiritual capacities are sometimes recognized, valued, and cultivated or given the space in which the child might cultivate them, but at other times, they are not recognized and therefore not valued as essential to being human. In some instances, these capacities are recognized but not valued, or perhaps even seen as troublesome or threatening. In more sinister instances, these capacities are used as a means of exploitation, such as in the indoctrination of children into belief systems that are harmful to them. After recognition of the value—perhaps even the sacred value—of the spiritual nature of children, the next most important role of the adult in the spiritual life of the child is to engage with the child in these capacities. This speaks to the relational nature of spirituality—it is dependent on relational context for its development (Myers, 1997).

In addition to conceptualizing spirituality or the spiritual as a particular type of experience it is also helpful to conceptualize it as integral to all experience, whether it is the specific focus of the experience or not. If our spiritual nature is that which makes us most fully human then our entire existence is infused with this quality of being. In children, spirituality and spiritual development are then seen as integral to growth and development, but spirituality also serves an integrating function. The meaning making involved in spirituality helps the child to put together a working model of (or perspective on) life that serves the purpose of furthering her development.

**An example of nurturing the spiritual life of the child.** Montessori included in her Cosmic Education curriculum a special lesson called "The Long Black Strip," which I gave a number of times during my tenure as a Montessori teacher. This lesson makes use of a 200 foot long, 6 inch wide black strip of cloth with a half-inch piece of bright red fabric at the very end of the strip. With the red strip as the starting point, the fabric is rolled into a large, black wheel, hiding the red strip in the very center. When hearing the story of "The Long Black Strip" for the first time, the children gathered for the lesson do not know that the center contains that thin red strip on the end of the fabric. The teacher or "guide" then tells the story of the evolution of life on earth while slowly unrolling the fabric during the telling. Because the strip is so long, the story is typically told outdoors where the full length of the strip can be unrolled in a straight line. The story is told around the theme of every life form having its own purpose that contributes to life's evolution. Briefly, in the very beginning, the sea lilies filter the water in the too-salty sea, making it less salty; this prepares the water for other life forms to evolve within it, which means sea creatures then proliferate. Later, lichen "learn" to grow on land and produce oxygen in order that plant life on land can evolve. Some sea creatures learn to use oxygen, preparing the way for amphibians. Amphibians make way for the reptiles, and from reptiles birds evolve, until finally mammals evolve. Rather than laying eggs in a protective shell, mammals learn the very special way of reproducing by protecting their young in a womb within their own bodies.

The plot of this story involves the forward movement of life on earth toward more diverse, complex, and interdependent existence of all life. The forward movement is accomplished by life forms "learning" something that allows for a new life form to evolve. In this way, each life form has its own purpose that contributes to the whole as the whole becomes ever more interdependent, evolved, and wonder-ful to contemplate. The climax in the telling of this story is when that final turn of fabric is unrolled to reveal the relatively tiny red strip representing human beings at the end of a very long evolutionary process. This graphically portrays how long it took life on earth to evolve to the point where human beings appeared. This point, however, is not spoken to the children; it is simply allowed to make an impression on the children. The children will also have the experience of walking alongside the black strip as it unfolds, feeling the dramatic difference in length between the long black portion of it compared with the thin red portion by the number of steps they take while following the story.

Leaving the story at the end without explanation of the meaning of the red strip, and without asking the question that might be hanging in the air—what then, is *our* purpose as human beings— allows these impressions to to have an effect and allows these questions to arise in the children, without the adult muddying the spiritual ground in which the children experience the story. If explanations were given by the adult at this significant moment, the focus would shift from the child's own embodied experience to the adult's analysis, interpretation, and evaluation of the content of the lesson. Thus silence on the part of the adult after telling the story is crucial to the learning experience of the child. If the children ask questions at this moment or make comments on their impressions of the strip or the story they have just heard, the adult then engages with the child where the child is in her understanding. If the child comments on something that seems irrelevant to the story, the guide does not correct or try to force the child to experience what she wants him to experience, but simply remains present, curious, and available for the child's pondering, contemplating, expressing, or questioning. The adult does not presume to know the ways in which the child is putting things together for herself; what might seem like an irrelevant question to the adult might be very logical in terms of the child's unique learning process.

The content of Montessori's Long Black Strip lesson and the way in which the lesson is given address one of the prominent aspects of the spiritual life of the child: how we make sense of our existence and how we contribute to that meaning by participating in it. If, in this lesson, the purpose of life is for us to move forward as an interdependent, ever-evolving whole, the child might wonder about the role of human beings in this whole. From this wondering, the child might begin to consider what her own role might be—what are her gifts and how might she contribute to society and to life. She might transcend her own boundaries in seeing herself as connected to and a part of something greater than herself. Therefore, the spiritual capacities of wonder and wondering, as well as the spiritual process of meaning-making and perhaps even transcendence may all be a part of this special lesson.

The lesson of The Long Black Strip is an example of nurturing the spiritual life of the child simply because it engages the spiritual nature of the child. The lesson is not designed to further any particular belief system but rather to tap into that spiritual state of wondering and contemplation. This demonstrates the idea that a child's spirituality is more like the building block of her existence than it is an aspect of existence. This also speaks to the point that spiritual development "though a unique stream of human development—cannot be separated from other aspects of one's being" (Roehlkepartain, et al., 2008, p. 4). Thus spirituality is integral to the child's development while also being its own line of development.

**The integrating function of spirituality.** During childhood, the child's spiritual capacities serve to help integrate the "threads of meaning" (Hyde, 2008, p.117) into a personally meaningful experience of herself in the world. This includes the spiritual capacities previously discussed, in addition to the capacity for faith. With faith operating integral to the meaning making process, the child may develop a sense of meaning and purpose inclusive of a spiritual world view. With a spiritual world view, spiritual life then becomes movement toward Ultimate Unity (Hyde, 2008) with personal challenges being put into the framework of a spiritual perspective. Even when the child is too young to verbally construct meaning, the experiences of development contribute to the spiritual life of the child, as spirituality contributes to the experiences of development. There is reciprocal interaction between experience and spirituality. Myers (1997) pointed out that even from infancy, human beings have an "innate human desire to climb over or move beyond . . . [which] is a process of transcendence" (p. 10). Again, this is another demonstration of the way in which spirituality is interwoven in the developmental process. Although some of the experiences of transcendence are not what we typically refer to as "spiritual" experience, in general, any experience of transcendence is on the continuum of experiences that potentially contribute to an individual's spiritual growth process. Moving beyond oneself in transcendent experiences can be anything from learning to grasp the rattle as an infant to transcending the personal self in a transpersonal experience of cosmic consciousness or universal love. These are all experiences of self-transcendence. Spirituality then, serves to integrate meaning and experience in such a way that opens up a path toward connection with whatever one perceives to be the source of all existence. It is the process of making sense of oneself, the world, and life.

Spirituality is relational in that it is the bond of connection with oneself, others, and the transcendent or the transpersonal Self. Clearly, all human beings who survive infancy have had a base of relational experience, whether this was fully engaged, attuned parenting or being left in a crib in an orphanage. Being left in a crib would be a base of experience notable for the absence of engagement rather than the quality of engagement. Nonetheless, this base of experience sets the stage for future intrapsychic, interpersonal, and transpersonal relations and sets the stage for the process of spiritual development.

In the literature reviewed for this study, it seems to me that when the self is taken into consideration from the point of view of the person as subject, not object, spirituality has to do with the person's orientation to self, others, and the world. The sense of self is infused with the person's spirituality—it is not a separate aspect of being, it is beingness itself. It is true there may be some people who take an active interest in spirituality itself, but that which "propels the search for connectedness, meaning, purpose, and contribution" (Benson et al., 2003, pp. 205-206) can be discussed as spiritual in nature regardless of whether these meanings, purposes, and sense of connectedness are attributed to the divine or the sacred. The capacities for wonder, awe, and wisdom, or the sensitivities such as awareness sensing or mystery sensing are spiritual, yes, but they are part of the natural function of the spiritual nature of beingness. When we consider our physical and psychological interdependence with the rest of humanity, this gives way to the fundamentally spiritual nature of human existence. It is only when human beings are not regarded as human beings, but as objects, that we miss this. It is only when, in our imagination we think about grand questions such as how to educate millions of people that we become perhaps overwhelmed in thinking about the number of people as objects and we start to think we need a machine to educate them. It is only when metaphors from nature are replaced by metaphors from industry and technology that we collapse our perspective on humanity and see human beings as things to be run through an assembly line or as "consumers" and that we lose sight of the naturally spiritual nature of our existence.

**The spiritual as an integral feature of the psychological.** In contrast to developmental perspectives, the Jungian perspective on the psyche offers an integrated model of the spiritual and the psychological. Rather than framing spirituality as an aspect of psychological development, the Jungian perspective sees the human psyche as fundamentally spiritual; the relation between the ego (the self) and the Self is integral to the overall psychological picture of human beings. Assagioli (1976) also depicts the relation between the ego and the transpersonal Self as fundamental to psychological functioning. There does not exist a clear separation and distinction between the psychological and the spiritual; rather, the spiritual is a central organizing feature of the human psyche. Thus from these perspectives there is less distinction between psychological development and spiritual development than there is in most developmental perspectives. This is particularly important when considering the role of spirituality in the development of a sense of self. Does spirituality have a role—is it a factor in the development of a sense of self, or is it the central condition of the self? This will be addressed more fully later in the study.

*Chapter Six*


# The Human-Nature Connection


Nature seemed to me full of wonders, and I wanted to steep myself in them. Every stone, every plant, every single thing seemed alive and indescribably marvelous.

Jung, 1961/1989, p. 32


In reviewing the literature on the human-nature connection particularly with regard to children, it was clear that the "voice of the earth" (Roszak, 2001) persistently calls us back to this relationship in the context of present day scholarship and culture. Authors from many different fields have addressed this relationship in the apparent need to make reparations in our sense of disconnection from the earth. We have evidently become aware once again of the need to acknowledge the primacy of the human-earth relationship, almost as if we had forgotten the age-old wisdom that not only recognized this primacy but has made use of ritual, myth, and culture to express this recognition since the beginning of human existence. In the context of the current study, the findings on the human-nature connection have made themselves heard like the persistent beat of a drum maintaining rhythm in a song, or the beat of a heart, keeping time for the natural rhythms in the body. This "heart beat" seems to state, over and over again, that the human being and the earth are one.

## Human-Earth Unity

Demonstrating this unity, Roszak (2001) stated that as human beings we have our psychological roots in the natural world, as the "ecological unconscious"(p. 320). Wilson (1984) stated that the human mind originated in the matrix of living organisms that is the natural world around us. Jung described the continuity of the physical and the psychological with the phrase "unus mundus" which is a "transcendent, unitary existence"(Card, 1991). In this Jungian framework, the archetypes pattern everything within the unus mundus, from the matter of the physical world, to the mind of the psychological world. Berry (2006) drew attention to the "powers" of the earth and the sphere of human thought as one of these powers, which contributes to the furthering of greater Earth functioning. Finally, Macy (2007) described the earth as the greater Self of human existence, the Self within which the self of the individual exists. Macy also noted that individuals, "as *part* [emphasis added] of this world . . . contain the *whole* of it" (p. 28).

In the current study, Macy's (2007) perspective on the individual is important to emphasize, lest it sound as though there is no place for an individual self in the life of the earth as our greater Self. She stated,

> We don't have to surrender our individuality to experience the world as an extended self and its story as our own extended story. The liver, leg, and lung that are "mine" are highly distinct from each other, thank goodness, and each has a distinctive role to play. The larger "selfness" we discover today is not an undifferentiated unity. As in all living systems, intelligence depends on the integrative play of diversity. (p. 28)

## Earth-Human Unity As it Relates to the Child

In the unity that is the earth-human relationship, we can explore the particular significance of that relationship for the child. There is a two-fold significance in this relationship for the child: first, the child's development depends upon this relationship between human beings and the earth; and second, the relationship between human beings and the earth depends upon the child for its cultivation and reparation.

Clearly, it is well-known that time in the natural world has a positive impact on the child's development. Although this is not necessarily recognized in education policy or emphasized in developmental theory, data on the benefits for children of time in the outdoors is readily available. This is certainly relevant, but this is not the question being addressed in the current study. The more specific question of this study has to do with how a child's relationship with the natural world contributes to spiritual development and how this affects her sense of self. With the findings on children's spirituality and spiritual development having been articulated in the previous chapter, the findings on the child's relationship with the natural world may be stated with these in mind.

## The Child in the Natural World

The spiritual nature of the child includes special capacities, awarenesses, and experiences which are both cultivated by time in the natural world, and which allow for the sense of connection with the natural world. Kellert (2002, 2005) demonstrated that in addition to cognitive and moral development, the child's emotional receptivity and responsiveness are cultivated in engagement with the natural world. Emotional receptivity and responsiveness may then serve as the affective underpinnings of spiritual sensitivities and capacities. Wonder without emotional receptivity and responsiveness is a cognitive experience whereas wonder in concert with receptivity and responsiveness allows for the blossoming of the child's spiritual nature. Although Kellert did not discuss emotional receptivity and responsiveness as "spiritual," I make this connection based on the review of the literature and what seems to me to be the overlap between what these authors describe and what authors writing more specifically about children's spirituality describe. It is not as though Hart (2003) *excluded* the affective underpinnings of wonder and wondering or that Kellert (2002, 2005) *excluded* the spiritual aspect of emotional receptivity and responsiveness but rather that these authors address areas very closely connected with one another. Thus, in this connection it is possible to see how being in the natural world cultivates spiritual sensitivities and capacities, and how the spiritual nature of the child allows for the connection to the natural world that in turn cultivates emotional receptivity and responsiveness.

When the relationship between the child and the natural world is brought to the fore, those aspects of the child often left unattended in our test-happy society may be addressed. Rather than a focus on the cognitive acquisition of information, which is by default, the emphasis in many schools, the focus can shift to other capacities. As Berry put it in conversation with Carolyn Toben,

> the work is now in the realm of immanence. What is being lost today in western civilization is the development of soul capacities, which can lead us to our primary source of understanding within the mind, the imagination, and the emotions. The human-earth relationship can teach us to recover these through our unique human ability to reflect on the magnificence of a sunrise, the miracle of a humming bird, the profusion of blossoming flowers, the awesome sight of a waterfall, the lightning and thunder of the great storms. Through these outer experiences come our inner development and our creativity. (as cited in Toben, 2012, p. 82)

The "realm of immanence" is differentiated from the transcendent realm in the literature on the relationship between the child and the natural world. While James's view of the spiritual has traditionally been discussed more in terms of the transcendent, as in the work of Myers (1997), the literature on the human-earth connection emphasizes spiritual immanence in the natural world. The natural world is the immanent spiritual thus the phenomenological experience of the natural world cultivates the spiritual nature of the child as well as the "soul capacities" of which Berry spoke (as cited in Toben, 2012, p. 82).

As a soul capacity or subconscious faculty (Helminski, 1992), intuition also serves as a means of connection with the natural world. As a different way of knowing in contrast to analytical or scientific understanding, intuition allows an integrative way of knowing, making use of subtle faculties not easily parsed into identifiable mental functions. Jung (1928/1990) described intuition as "unconscious perception" (p. 214). Berry called intuition an "inner knowing" (as cited in Toben, 2012, p. 88). He further stated that "intuition is the unique quality of the human that is also the consciousness of the earth" (as cited in Toben, 2012, p. 88). In other words, intuition is one of the means of direct psychic connection between human beings and the earth. It is the innate, unconscious connection to the natural world. Berry cautioned that children lose this intuitive connection to the natural world "within a culture that doesn't understand or honor the intuition" (p. 88). He also recognized, however, that being in the natural world "activates" (p. 88) intuition within the child.

Robinson's (1983) work on the religious experience of childhood has several examples of how experiences in the natural world shape a child's future experience, activate intuition, and "become the basis for their thinking" (Toben, 2012). Again, Robinson (1983) reviewed the accounts told by adults of their earliest spiritual experiences, many of which took place in the natural world. One woman, age 57, recounted her experience as a 4 or 5-year-old girl walking on the moors with her mother. She wrote,

> As the sun declined and the slight chill of evening came on, a pearly mist formed over the ground. My feet, with the favourite black shoes with silver buckles, were gradually hidden from sight until I stood ankle deep in gently swirling vapour. Here and there just the very tallest harebells appeared above the mist. I had a great love of these exquisitely formed flowers, and stood lost in wonder at the sight.
>
> Suddenly I seemed to see the mist as a shimmering gossamer tissue and the harebells, appearing here and there, seemed to shine with a brilliant fire. Somehow I understood that this was the living tissue of life itself, in which that which we call consciousness was embedded, appearing here and there as a shining focus of energy in the more diffused whole. In that moment I knew that I had my own special place, as had all other things, animate and so-called inanimate, and that we were all part of this universal tissue which was both fragile yet immensely strong, and utterly good and beneficent. (as cited in Robinson, 1983, p. 32)

This beautiful account of an early spiritual experience was clearly stimulated by the young girl's sense of wonder at the beauty she experienced in the natural world. Not only did she have this experience some 50 years prior to this retelling, but the impact of the experience was so profound that the impression stayed with her throughout her life as she evidently continued to contemplate the nature of the experience. She continued,

> The vision never left me. It is as clear today as fifty years ago, and with it the same intense feeling of love of the world and the certainty of ultimate good. It gave me then a strong, clear sense of identity which has withstood many vicissitudes, and an affinity with plants, birds, animals, even insects, and people too, which has often been commented upon. Moreover, the whole of the experience has since formed a kind of reservoir of strength fed from an unseen source, from which quite suddenly in the midst of all the very darkest of times a bubble of pure joy rises through it all, and I know that whatever the anguish there is some deep centre in my life which cannot be touched by it.
>
> Of course, at the early age of four of five I could not have expressed anything of the experience in the words I have now used, and perhaps the attempt to convey the absorption of myself into the whole, and the intensity of meaning, sounds merely over-coloured to the reader. But the point is that, by whatever mysterious perception, the whole impression and its total meaning were apprehended in a single instant. . . . This is not the only experience of the kind that has come to me—indeed they occur relatively often—but it is without doubt the one which has laid the deepest foundations of my life, and for which I feel the profoundest gratitude. (as cited in Robinson, 1983, p. 33)

As stated in her account, she did not have the words to describe the experience as a child but only later, and with much contemplation of the experience, was she able to articulate her "absorption . . . into the whole"; however, even as an adult, she only "attempts to convey" the nature of the experience and "the intensity of meaning." Apparently, the experience was so profound that to accurately convey it with language had been very difficult.

In addition, this account makes clear the lifelong significance of the experience to this woman. It has a significant impact on her "sense of identity" and gave her "an affinity with plants, birds, animals, even insects, and people too" (as cited in Robinson, 1983, p. 32). Based on this account, this seems to have been an organizing experience for this woman.

Another example from Robinson's (1983) work conveys an attunement between a boy and the natural world around him. This was told by a 68-year-old man as he recollected his early life experience.

> Through the spring, summer and autumn days from about the age of seven, I would sit alone in my little house in the tree tops observing all nature around me and the sky overhead at night. I was too young to be able to think and reason in the true sense but with the open receptive mind of a young, healthy boy I slowly became aware of vague, mysterious laws in everything around me. I must have become attuned to nature. I felt these laws of life and movement so deeply they seemed to saturate my whole mind and body, yet they always remained just beyond my grasp and understanding. (as cited in Robinson, 1983, p. 32)

This speaks to what Berry described as a "deep intuition" (as cited in Toben, 2012, p. 63) and another way of "understanding through the heart" (as cited in Toben, 1983, p. 121). This man's description of how his intuitive understanding of the laws of nature "saturated" (as cited in Robinson, 1983, p. 32) his mind and body also speaks to Berry's discussion of immanence. The experience of observing nature for this man was felt within his own body, as an attunement to the natural world. Immanence also refers to the experience of the spiritual or divine within the natural world as was depicted in the first account by the woman who experienced "the living tissue of life itself" (as cited in Robinson, 1983, p. 32). Immanence is thus shared between the natural world and the child.

Another manifestation of the connection between children and the natural world is the experience of the unity of all of life. This is depicted in an account by a 46-year-old woman who clearly remembered having experienced this as a child but lost touch with this sense as she grew older:

> The only aspect in which I think my childhood experience was more vivid than in later life was in my contact with nature. I seemed to have a more direct relationship with flowers, trees and animals, and there are certain particular occasions which I can still remember in which I was overcome by a great joy as I saw the first irises opening or picked daisies in the dew-covered lawn before breakfast. There seemed to be no barrier between the flowers and myself, and this was a source of unutterable delight. As I grew older I still had a great love of nature and liked to spend holidays in solitary places, particularly in the mountains, but this direct contact seemed to fade, and I was sad about it. I was not quite able to grasp something which was precious. (as cited in Robinson, 1983, p. 49)

Another self-experience of the unity of all of life was recounted by a 44-year-old woman:

> My first remembered experience of the numinous occurred when I was barely three. I recall walking down a little cul-de-sac lane behind our house in Shropshire. The sun was shining, and as I walked along the dusty lane, I became acutely aware of the things around me. I noticed a group of dandelions on my left at the base of the stone wall. Most of them were in full bloom, their golden heads irradiated by the sun, and suddenly I was overcome by an extraordinary feeling of wonder and joy. It was as if I was part of the flowers, and stones, and dusty earth. I could feel the dandelions pulsating in the sunlight, and experienced a timeless unity with all life. It is quite impossible to express this in words, or to recall its intensity. All I know now is that I knew something profound and eternal then. Now I am deeply conscious that my human failings have taken me far from my childhood understanding of a greater reality. (as cited in Robinson, 1983, p. 49)

All of these accounts illustrate a profound sense of innate and intimate connection between the child and the natural world. Some of them suggest a later loss of the continued sense of connection or the loss of a continued sense of profound knowledge experienced in childhood. This draws attention to the child's unique capacity to experience a profound and intuitive sense of connection and attunement to the natural world. Whereas this capacity may remain intact throughout a person's life, the child's natural propensity for wonder and awe, or her spiritual nature predispose her to this kind of experience during childhood.

One final account of an early memory in relation to the natural world is provided by Jung (1961/1989) in *Memories, Dreams, Reflections*. He wrote,

> One memory comes up which is perhaps the earliest of my life, and is indeed only a rather hazy impression. I am lying in a pram, in the shadow of a tree. It is a fine, warm summer day, the sky blue, and golden sunlight darting through green leaves. The hood of the pram has been lifted up. I have just awakened to the glorious beauty of the day, and have a sense of indescribable well-being. I see the sun glittering through the leaves and blossoms of the bushes. Everything is wholly wonderful, colorful, and splendid. (p. 6)

As Jung's earliest memory, being told from his perspective some 80 years later, clearly, this memory comes from a foundational experience. Whether it is an accurate memory is not so much in question. The sensuous description of "indescribable well-being" recalled as his earliest memory speaks to his close identification with the natural world and a sense of self interwoven with his experience of well-being in the world around him.

## The Child as Important in the Reparation of the Human-Earth Relationship

Cobb's (1977) work influenced the findings on the child's relationship with the natural world and how this relationship figures into the questions of spirituality and sense of self development. Her work speaks to both aspects of the two-fold significance of the child's relationship with the natural world. She addressed both how this relationship and engagement with the natural world affects the child's development as well as how the child's development while engaged with the natural world shapes cultural evolution.

Starting with Cobb's (1977) recognition that "all knowledge . . . begins with sensory experience" (p. 53), she asserted that the child creates a world image through the sensory/perceptual experience of engagement with the natural world. The creation of this image, however, does not occur in a cultural vacuum; it occurs within a historical-cultural context. She wrote,

> A child is a human being, whose development is regulated by the meanings of nature imparted to him by the culture of his particular period in history, the particular mode in which he is taught to see and know himself in time and space.
>
> At one level of organization, this projective behavior is referred to as narrative or story; at another level, which evokes greater breadth and depth in time perspectives, it is identified as history. In this sense the roots of the human sense of history can be said to have emerged from the function of individual nervous systems. History in the spectrum of mind's relations with nature includes, at one extreme, self-history or autobiographical recall, which provides access to the earliest and most finite incidents. At the opposite extreme, mind continues to travel in search of further and further reaches of nature's history and biological evolution; thus biological development and cultural evolution become aspects of cosmic events. (pp. 51-52)

Here Cobb highlights the interpenetration of the child, the natural world, and the shaping of cultural evolution. This is where the reparation of the human-earth relationship through the child becomes apparent. When the child is further and further removed from the natural world, our cultural evolution is shaped in such a way that deepens the physical and psychological separation of human beings and the earth. We clearly see this with the greater use of electronics in place of outdoor play coinciding with greater cultural dysfunction and psychopathology. The alternative, however, would be to intentionally allow increased time in the natural world for the child but not only for the sake of the child; cultivating the child's connection to the natural world is a means of shaping cultural evolution in the direction of greater appreciation of the human-earth interdependence and reciprocity.

Cobb's (1977) work echoes Montessori's (1936/1966) statement that the way to cultivate peace is though the child. Rather than imposing on the child a condensed and simplified version of reality from the adult's perspective, the child is encouraged to meet his own God-given potential. In doing so, the child thereby co-creates a new, more peaceful vision of reality than that which could have been handed down by the teaching adult. One of the primary means of learning and meeting his own potential is through learning experiences based on or taking place in the natural world. The foundational and penultimate concept in the Montessori curriculum is the interdependency of all of life. Thus the idea is that the child is the frontier at which a new, more balanced and peaceful understanding of the world can be brought forth.

Returning to the wisdom of Berry, he made clear in his conversations with Toben that the child's relationship with the natural world is of critical importance. He explained:

> The child is growing up today in a geo-biological moment that has never before happened in sixty-five million years. The life of the child has always been *organized* . . . around a real abiding world of beauty, wonder and the intimacy of living processes—the wind, frogs, butterflies—not a manufactured electronic world of virtual reality.
>
> The child has a natural bond of intimacy with the natural world, a remarkable sense of identification with all living things. There is an ongoing common language between children and the earth; it is a language of living relationships.
>
> . . . Children need this deep personal connection with the natural world. . . . Out of these experiences they come to know something regarding the world, which becomes the basis for their thinking. (as cited in Toben, 2012, p. 96)

The findings from the review of literature on the human-earth relationship make it clear that not only do children "need this deep personal connection with the natural world" (Toben, 2012, p. 96) for their own sense of inner connection and development; in addition, we need to protect the child's natural propensity for deep personal connection with the natural world in order to repair the greater human-Earth relationship.

*Chapter Seven*

# Reflections From Within the Hermeneutic Circle

The academic work for this study began in an early research paper written in 2007. It was in this paper that I first explored the research on children's spirituality. At that time, the research on children's spirituality was just beginning to proliferate within academia. When I consider the personal dimension to this research process, however, the origins of this work go back well beyond graduate school, into my own childhood experiences and perhaps directly to the poem quoted at the start of this study which became a guidepost for me in my life. Throughout the course of graduate school and while conducting this study, I have relived many childhood experiences and brought to my memory of them a new perspective—that of the meaning-seeking adult.

In working with the personal dimension of the work and attempting to understand my own complex ties to the work, there was a process of reflecting on my experiences in engaging "the work" beyond the bounds of the research process itself. It has only been in retrospect that some of the pieces have fallen into place, revealing a persistent call to the work and seemingly the work's own orchestrations. This became clear in reviewing papers I had written as explorations of the imaginal approach to research, what I might bring to the work, as well as the topic itself.

## Being Called to the Work

As mentioned in the introduction to this study, I entered graduate school with a question about children's spirituality steeping within me. My childhood spiritual experiences seemed to have greatly impacted my own sense of self, and this was at the heart of my questions about children's spirituality and sense of self development; however, I also was "called" to another aspect of the work through Carolyn Toben and her invitation to take part in the Inner Life of the Child in Nature (ILCN) program at The Center for Education, Imagination and the Natural World (CEINW). Somehow not only spirituality and sense of self were to be a part of the work, but this third element, the role of the natural world, seemed to almost forcibly push its way into the picture. Again, as mentioned in the Introduction, I received a call to participate in the work of CEINW in exactly the month I was to begin graduate studies at Pacifica. Against my protestations that I would probably not have time for such an endeavor, Carolyn insisted that I could do both—that it would not demand too much of my time. In considering how Carolyn and I had met, the immediate connection I sensed with her, as well as the chance meeting with old friends after not having seen them for a couple of years that put Carolyn and me in touch in the first place, I decided this was a "call" I should probably heed.

Since the research process would not begin in earnest until much later, I completed the ILCN program before my topic was clearly defined. The impact of this work at CEINW and the synchronous nature of the call to that work led me to find a way to weave this into the study. There was a strong sense of loyalty to my original question as well as to the work I had been introduced to at CEINW. Thus rather than working with only sense of self and spirituality, I found myself working on how to integrate the natural world into this study.

When I initially "chose" this topic, it was unclear to me how my own wounding might have called me to the work. In fact, I questioned whether it was too benign a topic that would not result in depth-ful work. I articulated these questions in an exploratory journal response I wrote in 2009 after reading *The Wounded Researcher* (Romanyshyn, 2007):

> My experience in coming up with my research topic has been that I was unaware of the ways in which my own wounds have probably called me to the work. I didn't realize and probably still don't fully realize that part of the draw to my topic has been some of my own personal wounds, in addition to wounds on other levels. In fact, at times I have wondered if perhaps I was choosing a topic that was too safe, too clean and pretty to

be worthy of several year's work. I'm not finished constructing my research question but I am interested in spirituality as it contributes to the development of a sense of self and the embeddedness of spirituality in nature. I continue to feel drawn to this work and have had some signs of encouragement that this was a "good" direction to go in but when I am somewhat removed from the topic, it sounds a bit fluffy. "Spirituality" is such a trendy topic and the question of its relevance in the life of children almost seems like it should be discussed over tea and crumpets with wealthy parents whose children are in elite prep schools. . . . But something tells me there may be more to this topic than I can now detect. Something tells me perhaps I have been blind to my own wounding within the context of this topic, and something tells me that perhaps this connects with a level of wounding that isn't so pretty and fluffy. (Author's log book, February 20, 2009)

Another component of this process of being called to the work was my struggle with the seeming incongruousness of contemplating this topic in the midst of working with incarcerated adolescent boys. The boys in this setting seemed to have nothing further from their minds than a spiritual connection with the natural world. From the same response journal, this excerpt demonstrates how puzzling this was for me at that time:

The dark shadow in the back of my mind when I write about this is the reminder that for my practicum I have been working with primarily African American adolescent boys who are incarcerated. Why does this shadow come to mind when I think about my topic? What does the question of spirituality have to do with boys who have had to basically struggle for their lives in a state of poverty and neglect? Isn't a more relevant question for them how to survive in society without being killed or ending up in prison?

Right now there exists a chasm between the world of the boys I work with and my quaint research topic that I came up with at a graduate school in a setting that couldn't be more of an antithesis to the setting these boys grew up in. Lovely gardens, picturesque southern California, an abundance of wealth and opportunity. . . . These are the things I think of in relation to Pacifica when I consider the backgrounds of my current clients. But perhaps below the bridge that connects these two worlds within me and within our culture, there is more to be discovered. That is where I guess I'll have to head next in development of my topic.

But here's another thing: (right now I see this as irony but perhaps my perspective will change as I get into the trans- ference dialogs and the field of the transference) the setting where I am doing my practicum is actually a large campus in a rural area of the piedmont of North Carolina, where there are no sounds of traffic and not much development. It takes me about 40 minutes to drive there and along the way I drive past old farmhouses and barns, a large lake, several small ponds and some very scenic, if culturally rural, areas. It's a pleasant drive most of the way and nature, as opposed to develop- ment, predominates. Once I arrive at the "youth development center" where I work, there's a long driveway up a low-grade hill through the trees to the parking lot and main facility. The campus is surrounded by 18-foot fences with razor wire on inward-curving extensions at the top. Inside the fenced area, there are winding paths connecting the "cottages" where the boys reside. The spaces between the buildings are populated with tall oaks, like sentries standing about the campus. Birds, squirrels, even some cats, all play a part in making this an odd admixture of natural beauty and pain. It's sad to know that the boys inside the buildings have no ability to connect with the nature around them, if for no other reason than they are not permitted to be outside except when being walked like a chain gang from one building to the next.

Isn't it strange that one of the principle aspects to my topic is *nature* and that, in contrast to the population with whom I am working, my work place is embedded in a rather beautiful, (if somewhat neglected and untended) natural setting? For a while I considered changing my whole topic because the question of spirituality seemed so incongruous with the work I was doing with so many gang-involved, neglected people: the castaways of our society. But the original question kept pulling me back so I decided to stick with it; yet I continue to be more and more immersed in the work at the youth development center where the topic doesn't seem that relevant. Except when I open my eyes to the natural surroundings. (Author's log book, February 20, 2009)

Another surprising aspect of this particular call to the work is the circumstances of how I ended up working at a youth development center in the first place. In my efforts to arrange my first practicum experience I had called numerous agencies, clinics, and service providers. For quite some time, however, I was unable to procure a practicum placement. After a period of time long enough for me to have forgotten having called the clinical director at the youth development center, she called me, seemingly out of the blue, and asked if I wanted to come in for an interview. Although I had notes on calls made and lists of the agencies I had contacted, I never found my record of having called that particular facility. I have no doubt I did call despite not remembering or finding a record of it, but the fact that this was the place I ended up working is, once again, like a reminder of how the work itself seems to orchestrate its own doing.

As I discovered only later in the study, it was exactly that which seemed to me to be the "incongruousness" between my topic and my work with incarcerated youth that later proved to be an entry point into the deeper levels of the work. It was also the incongruousness of the beautiful natural setting in which the "junior prison" was situated that had me puzzling over the relation of the natural world to the other facets of the study. From the beginning, this served to put me in Keats's state of negative capability, in which I had the sense of not knowing what the work was about and not knowing how my own experiences figured into the work itself. If I had not literally been called to work in the youth development center, I might not have had a question opened within me as to the meaning of the work in the context of children whose lives had clearly not started out well. Although I can now see this in retrospect, during the period this question surfaced within me, it was not at all clear that this was part of the process of the unfolding of the work. Although I was mindful of the autonomous nature of the work, my experience at the time was that these questions had to do more with my own limitations as a scholar than with the work itself. I certainly sensed the "pull" of the work but the state of mental uncertainty I found myself in was a state I had grown accustomed to labeling as being "dumb." Fortunately I had already developed a fair tolerance of this state, seemingly as my only option since it occurred with relative frequency. It is only in retrospect and in the stance of honoring the alchemical hermeneutic method that, rather than labeling this state with self-diminishing language, I can allow that this "dumbness" might actually be useful, acceptable, and a meaningful part of an intuitive way of knowing. Though the fantasy of fact-based, "objective" knowing would have me believe certainty should be my constant companion throughout the research process, the inclusion of an intuitive way of knowing recognizes that when the mind does not "know" with certainty, other faculties of the human psyche are free to participate in a more integrative form of knowledge.

This background is simply a depiction of the interplay between myself as researcher and the work itself. This interplay only became clear in retrospect. It is an example of what Romanyshyn (2007) described as being called to the work. This experience was a part of the process of choosing the topic itself and an early demonstration of the particular ways in which I was "called" to the work.

## Conducting the Transference Dialogues

Once the topic was chosen, or I was "chosen" by the work, the research process itself has been its own unfolding. Not long after the above musings and in accord with my desire to take an imaginal approach to the research, it was time to attempt the transference dialogues and to more directly engage the unconscious levels of the work. When I did attempt the transference dialogues the results were surprising, revealing, and disturbing.

As the imaginal approach to research instructs, I prepared for the dialogues by *setting the stage*. In my preparations, I was inspired to set up an "altar" of sorts, a place where I could focus my energy and a place to go—it was a way of orienting myself in space although this was not a conscious thought at the time. I must have needed this kind of anchor in order to embark on this unknown voyage. I wandered around my house, looking for objects to place on the altar, objects that would be meaningful to me, that would help organize my energy for this process. I first found an empty Asian box with two doors on the front and a divided chamber within. A small piece of bamboo served to latch the doors together. This was the first object I chose as the centerpiece of the altar. I then selected several other small objects from around my house that represented different aspects of the work as previously identified. I also wrote the four questions as outlined in *The Wounded Researcher* (Romanyshyn, 2007) on index cards and taped them to the interior surfaces of the open box. With this done, I read the questions on the cards aloud, which is the second step in preparing for the dialogues, *sending out invitations.*

While *setting the stage* and *sending out invitations*, I was surrounded by family pets. My husband and I had two dogs, two cats, and a cockatiel at that time. Both dogs were with me while I made these preparations. The bird's cage was right behind me when I sat at my desk. Oddly, when I read the invitations aloud asking who the work serves, the animals seemed to become somewhat agitated. The bird began fluttering his wings and moving about in his cage and our small dog, Melia, began earnestly asking to be picked up. When I picked her up and placed her in my lap, she was shivering for some reason. At this point I decided to document this process by taking pictures of the altar and the animals.

The next step in preparing for the transference dialogues involves *waiting with hospitality.* In order to do this, I knew I would have to occupy my mind in some way, to decrease the vigilance with which I knew I would be watching for something to "happen." So I began to write a journal entry. I decided I would write down my musings and write about the process of *setting the stage, sending out invitations,* and *waiting with hospitality.* I started by writing the question: "Whom does the work serve?" Quickly and without thought, this was answered with: "The plants, trees, animals, all of creation. For when there is abuse, all are wounded." This response was surprising to me, as I had not been contemplating the subject of abuse in my musings on the research topic, nor had I considered the oneness of human beings and the natural world, which this statement seemed to suggest. Right after this, the journal entry shifts to a description of my bodily state: I was tired and my neck was aching. As I was paying attention to symptoms, I made note of these and explored what was being offered by these symptoms. I continued to write about the process of setting up the altar and the animals' reaction when I read the questions aloud. I made note of the weather, what I was seeing, the thoughts coming to mind and contemplations about their connection to my topic. Eventually, with nothing "happening" or no "visitation" seeming to occur, I concluded my work for the day.

The next night, I had a dream in which a fox appeared and seemed to want to make contact with me. My fear got in the way and I was hesitant in my dream to engage with him. When I awoke from this dream in the middle of the night, it had made a strong impression on me and although I wished to return to sleep I felt compelled to write it down.

On my next occasion to work, I sat down once again and, thinking I must not have been "doing" the transference dialogues "right" the last time I attempted them, I decided to just write questions with regard to the research topic, in hopes that writing questions would stimulate my thoughts and move me forward in crafting the work, even if the transference dialogues would not produce anything. In looking back at my writing for that day, it was then, after writing one of these questions, that my handwriting became markedly different. In this different handwriting, a series of very disturbing images were depicted: "*Dead people, dead children, children who have been hacked up brutally, children who have been abused, neglected, brutalized. Children who have been given away*" (Author's log book, March 16, 2009). This was followed by what seemed to be a direct response to my question as to whom the work served:

> *The work is for the child. The abused, neglected child, the aborted child, the abandoned child, the murdered child. The work gives voice to these children, who did not get to speak when they were living. The child who was not protected, not nurtured, not cared for in the way the child expects to be cared for. . . . The child wants to speak.* (Author's log book, March 16, 2009)

At this point I asked, in writing, what "the child" wanted to say. This was answered with:

> *The abandoned, neglected, abused child.*
>
> *There are so many things I would have told you if given the chance. . . . I had precious gifts to share, wisdom to impart, joy. But these were lost in the treacheries done upon me. . . . The flower that I was to become withered and died while still in bud. I want you to unfold me. Love me into existence. Love the stillborn blossom within the shriveled bud into existence to hear what I meant to say. It won't be easy. The writing will unfold petal upon petal but I am like a peoni with many, many tightly packed petals, not like a tulip with clean, well-defined petals. The writing will bring each petal forth to flower.* (Author's log book, March 16, 2009)

The dialogue continued in the voice of the child, stating that the child comes into being through being heard.[1]

> *A child wants to be heard. A child "speaks" herself into being but only becomes when she is heard. . . . When you listen to a child, you give the child a chance to come into being. . . . A child needs validation of being heard to come into being . . . . So many children have not come fully into being because they haven't been heard. The child is not an innocent. The child has wisdom and also brings darkness. But when children bring darkness, that too wants to be heard.* (Author's log book, March 16, 2009)

Once again a connection was made between the child and the natural world.

> *When there is neglect, abuse, trampling under foot, there is great damage to the child. The child is hurt, the child is wounded. The child, like nature, needs care, needs to be heard, needs to be treasured.* (Author's log book, March 16, 2009)

---

[1] For a full transcript of the transference dialogues, please see Appendix 1

The experience of engaging in these dialogues was tiring and I soon found myself asleep on the desk in front of me. Through all of the coursework I had done in my doctoral program, this was the first time I had ever fallen asleep on my desk.

These transference dialogues, as mentioned, were quite shocking as it seemed this material came out of nowhere. Not only were the images incredibly disturbing, the direct connection between abuse of the child and abuse of the natural world was an entirely new idea to me. I could not recall anywhere in my conscious memory having made this kind of connection before. Even conceptualizing environmental destruction as abuse was new to me.

I was not sure what to do with this material, as it seemed to be introducing an entirely new angle on the topic which I was hesitant to incorporate. It seemed to be opening up the question of child abuse in relation to the natural world. With three major facets to the study already identified, introducing yet another enormous area of investigation was incomprehensible. As I explored this prospect further, however, I realized that the work was not to be about abuse *per se*. Intuitively, I was not led further in this direction. The research I did, the materials I read, the unconscious contributions through dreams, symptoms, and synchronicities did not encourage further pursuit of the topic of child abuse the way the other aspects of my topic seemed to have been encouraged by unconscious contributions or other sources of wisdom. I therefore let go of the idea that perhaps my topic needed to change. This was a difficult decision to make since it brought into question just how reliable my intuition is in relation to the research process. What if I took the work in the wrong direction or did not do what I was supposed to do? The uncertainty, I soon found, was to remain with me as a prominent feature of the entire research process.

**Listening to dreams.** Some time after these transference dialogues, I had another dream that seemed to be directly related to the work and was a significant contribution from the imaginal approach to research. The dream was a vivid depiction of the interpermeation (W. Adams, 1999) between the child and the natural world. It also put me in touch with an aspect of my own wounding and helped me see its connection with the work.

I was in a grocery store. Suddenly, a young girl, probably about 7 years old, ran into the store. I couldn't see her face or any really distinguishing characteristics other than that she was extremely *wild*. Her movement was wild, untamed, and unpredictable, and her appearance was also wild. She was clothed, I believe, but somehow the idea was that she had literally grown up in the wild, as if she had been raised by wolves.

In the dream, when I saw her I was stunned, as was everyone in the store, that she made an appearance. She was running around the store like crazy and then for some reason she ran and sat on my lap. . . . I couldn't fathom why she would do such a thing, based on where she was coming from. I somehow got the idea that I needed to take her into my care and, with trepidation, decided to do so. The last thing I remember is driving away with her in a car. We both seemed to be in the back seat of the car and the car itself represented where she had come from. The car was dark brown and looked like it had been sitting, abandoned out in the woods for years and years. . . . But it was fairly pleasant in there, almost pastoral, with brilliant sunlight shining on a slightly fluttering mound of loose leaves in the back seat. It was as if the car had been at rest for a long, long time and nature was simply taking its course around and in it. As we drove away in this vehicle, again there was a witnessing presence in the form of what seemed to be a black man, like an elderly grocer of a country store, who marveled or wrinkled his brow, that I would attempt to take her home with me. I knew this was not going to be easy. (Author's log book, July 2, 2009)

In this case, the "wild child" seemed to be both an aspect of myself—an abandoned part of me, feeling left alone as if to be "raised by wolves," as well as an aspect of the child herself. She also perhaps represented the natural, "untamed" or in other words, unspoiled and undomesticated, child who is deeply connected to the natural world—a part of it, in fact. Why did this child come to me in the dream? Was it a healing—reclaiming a lost part of myself? Was it a depiction of the relation between the conscious and unconscious aspects of myself, suggesting in this case, a collaboration between the the two in this work? Was it a depiction of the way the adult and the child would each give to the other? In the dream, I was in her car so in a sense she was taking me with her, but as the adult, I was taking her with me as well. Did the wild child come to sit on my lap, as if perhaps she might speak to me, or invite me into her world because I had "heard" in the transference dialogues that "the child wants to speak"? What was the concern on the part of the grocer as to what it would mean to take her into my care? Was I to "tame" her, take her out of the natural world? Or was it rather that she had some work to do on me?

In the course of reviewing the literature on children's spirituality, sense of self development, and the human-nature connection, I had the persistent feeling of being overwhelmed by the enormity of the three bodies of literature, to the point that I frequently found myself saying "I can't do this." My complex ties to the work seemed to recreate a childhood state of confusion, overwhelm, and the internalization of self-diminishing statements such as "I don't have anything to say" or "I'm not intelligent enough to do this" or "I don't know what I'm doing" or "what is wrong with me that this is so difficult?" The research process has been its own wilderness experience, complete with the sense of being left alone and "raised by wolves." The wolves in this case were perhaps in the form of intuitive guidance, without which, I believe I would not have been able to complete the process. (Maybe the dream of the fox after initially *sending out invitations* was one of these "wolves.") Although this regressed state was not pleasant to experience—was actually quite disorienting at times and often threatened to sabotage the study, it was useful as a means of bringing consciousness to the state of childbeing. This was not self-reflection and analysis of what was going on but the phenomenological recreation of the particular wounding I had experienced and carried with me since childhood, perhaps as the historic legacy of "the child" in my family and my ancestors. This was likely the source of the unconscious pull to the work. Once again, as a researcher conducting psychological research using alchemical hermeneutics, these experiences and the revelations I gained from them were tied to the autonomous nature of the work. My task then, was to discover the relevance of these revelations to children in the context of the study.

The process of utilizing my own experience, thoughts, reflections, dreams, synchronicities, and symptoms in conjunction with the material I was studying, brought a fullness and richness to my understandings about the relationship between self, spirituality, and the natural world in children. Although I struggled greatly with the challenge of incorporating all three aspects into this study and often considered elininating one of them, it was very clear that bringing all three elements into the discussion had its own purpose. Conducting research using the alchemical hermeneutic method meant that there were many moments of reverie, many synchronicities, and many engagements with the "others" in the work. To give a complete chronicle of these experiences would not serve the purposes of this study; rather, it would overwhelm and dilute the relevant findings. A few of these experiences, however, were particularly influential during the research process and directly affected the unfolding of the study. Others were like whispered secrets; I struggled to hear them but they silently kept their secret guarded until the right moment. The following are examples of this kind of participation from the unconscious during the research process.

## Working With Productions from the Unconscious and Scholarly Amplification

Early in the research process, while contemplating the stubborn fact that there were to be three aspects to the study, I began playing with graphic depictions of the interrelationship between self, spirituality, and the natural world. Drawing on the notion that the Star of David represents the interpenetration of the divine and the earthly (or in my rendition, the spiritual and the natural world) I began drawing this graphic in various ways. Eventually this led to contemplation of what would happen to this graphic if the third dimension (the self) were added to it, making the triangles into pyramids, hence the three-dimensional form of interpenetrating pyramids. This experience of falling into reverie was, in retrospect, like an "abduction" (Romanyshyn, 2007), in that an entire day in the library became consumed by contemplating the shape of the space that would be created in the interior between the two pyramids where they penetrated one another.

In my mind, this was simply a geometric puzzle that I thought would help me understand the relationships between self, spirituality, and the natural world. Had I not "lost myself" in these contemplations, I certainly would have questioned the wisdom of spending my time in this way. This was so compelling, however, that it was almost as if I had no choice but to be consumed by these contemplations. I had never before encountered two interpenetrating pyramids, at least not to my conscious recollection, and working with the spatial aspect of this apparently put me in that state of flow wherein time is lost.

I envisioned the natural world as the bottom pyramid, spirituality as the top pyramid, and the self as the place in between. Somehow it seemed to me that using the metaphor of the interpenetrating pyramids would help me penetrate the meaning and significance of the relationship between human beings, the earth, and the spiritual. I was compelled to find a graphic depiction of the interpenetrating pyramids and after searching online for quite a long time, I finally found one. It was a photograph of a crop circle. This I found astonishing, just to consider the possibility that there might be some greater meaning to this beyond my own musings. I was simply looking for geometric shapes to represent that which I was trying to put into words. The discovery of the photograph of the crop circle signaled to me that this was more than an instructional graphic that I had somehow "invented." The exact significance, however, remained elusive and I had no choice but to conclude my work for the day.

That afternoon, after such an immersion in the imagery of the Star of David and the interpenetrating pyramids, I found it difficult to leave the contemplative, imaginal realm and reconnect with my surroundings. Fortunately, I had my much needed, weekly yoga class to attend, which put a boundary on these musings and served to ground me again. Within 30 minutes, I was sitting cross-legged on the mat facing a large, hand-painted tapestry depicting the seven chakras and the yoga asanas representing them. I just happened to sit directly in front of, and at eye level with the fourth chakra or heart chakra, represented by the Star of David, which I had never before noticed. This was somewhat startling but invited further contemplation of this symbol. I realized that the fourth chakra is the center chakra— as mentioned, the heart chakra, and if one extended the lines of the downward pointing triangle up into the sky, and extended the lines of the upward pointing triangle down into the earth, the center of the symbol would be the human heart—the connecting point between "heaven" and earth. Somehow it seemed that the center of the human being is at the centerpoint between heaven and earth, between the psyche and the soma, the spiritual and the physical, the earthly and the divine.

Because I did not know exactly what to do with this in terms of how spirituality affects the child's development of a sense of self and what role the natural world plays in this process, I simply let it sit. It was not for quite a long time—in fact, not until I began writing about this experience, that I found more information on interpenetrating pyramids in the 17th-century work of physician and alchemist Robert Fludd:

> The central image that appears in many of Fludd's engravings, and that is reiterated over and over in his writings as the basis of his entire philosophy: [is] the interpenetrating pyramids. . . . The pyramids represent an opposing dualism: light and darkness, forma and materia. All beings constitute a proportionate mixture of forma and materia., and the point lying exactly between the extremities of the pyramidal basis is the equilibrium or sphaera aequalitatis. (Vickers, 1986, p. 190)

How is it that what I now recognize as the archetypal image of the interpenetrating pyramids came to me in connection with this work? How is it that the meaning I made from this form was so closely aligned with a 17th-century physician who wrote about "the inter-relation of God with the natural and human world?" (p. 190). Is this in fact relevant to the current study?

This process, as described above, is part of the scholarly amplification involved in the imaginal approach to research. The image or archetype of the interpenetrating pyramids could be considered a production from the unconscious. Clearly, with its archetypal nature and the evidence of it in the work of Fludd, this was not something that I produced from my own individual imagination. When the image presented itself I was given the opportunity to engage the unconscious level of the work—a level beyond the first level of my own personal unconscious. Following the surfacing of this image, a scholarly investigation takes place in order to find connecting points between that which was produced from the unconscious and the topic itself.

## Early Whispered Secrets Eventually Revealed

Even earlier in the research process than the above account of the "abduction" into reverie about the interpenetrating pyramids, there was an instance I now understand as being like an early whispered secret told to me in connection with this work. This "secret" was "told" in June of 2010. I only finally understood or heard the secret, or it only revealed itself to me in December of 2012, this morning in fact.

While reading the morning paper over breakfast on June 11, 2010, I came across a photograph and story that moved me deeply. The photograph in particular was especially moving. I cut out this story with the photograph and took pains, for some reason I do not recall, to include the newspaper folio, which is where the name, date, and name of the newspaper appear at the top of each page. I folded this clipping in such a way as to not crease the photograph and I put it in my office in one of the ever-present piles on my desk.

This morning, I was searching for a book in the bureau in my office. I came across, once again, the faded newspaper clipping from Raleigh *The News and Observer* on June 11, 2010. Many times, as I have cleaned, organized, and reorganized my office, piled, filed, and purged the papers that seem to accumulate there, I have come across this clipping. Many times I have chided myself for keeping this clipping, not knowing why I thought I must keep it and not knowing what to do with it. Should I frame the photograph? Should I file it? Why should I keep it and what would I do with it? With these questions remaining unanswered, the clipping survived, hiding in piles, being rescued from the recycle bin on second thought at least two or three times. I actually did not give it much thought that this clipping stuck around but just considered this as one of the many ways I sometimes seem a mystery to myself.

The clipping shows a photograph (see Appendix) thought to be taken in the early 1860's of two African American boys. The finding of this photo in the attic of a deceased man, was reported in the newspaper for being such a rare photograph, taken in 1862. The boys in the photo are dressed in torn, ragged clothing, barefoot, and sitting on a barrel. One of the boys is very sullen and angry looking, whereas the other looks more like he is slightly bewildered, perhaps somewhat compliant. They are slave boys. The angry boy, named John, sold for $1,150 in 1854. The bill of sale for the boy was found with the photograph, in safe keeping of a man thought to be a descendent of John.

This morning, I decided to take this clipping with me when I prepared to work. After all this time, I was pleased I kept this clipping but still did not know quite what to do with it. Looking into the eyes of the children sitting on the barrel, I could see the pain, anger, and confusion, and the lovable child hiding behind them. I began pondering whether this might have been, once again, the orchestrations of The Work. I searched my journal writings to see if I wrote anything about this when I read it in the newspaper back in 2010. I clearly remember reading the article in the paper and being so moved that I cut it out and saved it, but I never really understood what it meant to me or to my research. The pieces had not fallen into place yet. Would it, and *how* would it be a contribution to the research? After not finding anything in my writing about it, I read the article again for the first time since the day I first read it in the newspaper. It tells the story of the photograph itself but at the end it shifts to talking about the children in the photograph.

The story states that the collector who found the photograph is considering making a documentary about the boy, John, who was sold for $1,150. The final paragraph is a quote from the collector who was interviewed for the story. He said:

> This kid was abused and mistreated, and people forgot about him. He doesn't even exist in history. And to know that there were a million children who were like him. I've never seen another photo like that that speaks so much for children. (as cited in Norfleet, 2010, p. 3B)

The secret reveals itself. Now I understand why I could not just toss this clipping in the trash—not again. The Child would not be tossed in the trash and forgotten about one more time. Now the pieces fall into place and I understand why I was called to the work by the incarcerated

African American boys, quite possibly the direct descendents of slaves like John. This is the abandoned, neglected, and abused Child who wants to speak. This is the angry, sullen ragged child who hides within himself a loveable child, waiting to be heard, waiting to be loved into existence a petal at a time. This is who the work is for.

My earlier ponderings on the seeming incongruousness of incarcerated adolescent boys and the beautiful setting of the natural world was a sifting and shifting process, whereby the quandry itself prepared me for delving into the deeper levels of the unconscious. The ground of assumptions about what I thought I knew was rendered more fertile, more spacious in order for something unconscious and unknown to emerge. The spaces between the pieces of the puzzle did not seem to accommodate the pieces that belonged there until the contributions from the unconscious rearranged my perspective. A new perspective has become clear where the incongruous is now congruous and the whole picture has emerged. *For when there is abuse all are wounded.*

## The Alchemical Hermeneutic Method Used in Conjunction With Traditional Research Methods

The hermeneutic method used in the review of the literature was not enough, by itself, to make the kind of connections and interpretations offered in the alchemical hermeneutic method and imaginal approach to research. The voices in the literature revealed a great deal about the topic; however, the full integration of all three aspects of the topic could not, apparently, occur without the contributions from the unconscious. The idea and image of the interpenetrating pyramids, the text that came in the transference dialogues, the dream of the wild child, the synchronous events such as starting Pacifica and receiving the call from Carolyn Toben, as well as the whispering secrets that finally revealed themselves, are all contributions from the unconscious that have guided and greatly impacted the research process. These contributions allow a wholeness, the integration of conscious and unconscious, that is not possible when research is conducted without the engagement of the unconscious during the research process. The full elaboration of specifically how these guided and impacted the research process takes place in the following chapter.

## Research with Soul in Mind as Personal Transformation

As discussed in the chapter on methodology, the alchemical hermeneutic method is a both a research method and a potentially transforming experience for the researcher when deep subjectivity is used to both penetrate and be penetrated by the work itself. When approaching research in this way, there is a loss of differentiation between researcher and work, such that the researcher loses him or herself in the work, followed by a subsequent differentiation between what one brings to the work and the work itself (Romanyshyn, 2007). As noted, my experience during the research process entailed just this kind of loss of differentiation between myself and the work to the point that I "became," in many ways, the child about which I was writing. (Fortunately, there was also a subsequent differentiation between what I brought to the work and the work itself such that I was able to reclaim my adult status relatively intact.) Throughout the research process, several significant dreams occurred which serve as mile markers, so to speak, of the transformation as it occurred.

The Dream of the Wild Child was a dream which foretold the personal reclaiming of a lost part of myself as well as a tableau representing important themes for the work. A year later, during the weekend I attended my 99-year-old grandmother's funeral, I had another striking dream. In this dream, which I now call "The Abyss," I drove in a car along a hilly mountaintop area. It was dark out and suddenly I found I was not driving on the road but over grassy terrain. In an instant, I had driven over a cliff and found myself plungeing at breakneck speed into an abyss. The experience in the dream was terrifyingly real and I felt I was about to meet my end. Breathtaking terror was my first reaction but when it was clear I had no means of saving myself from this fate, I realized my only option was to be present and still within myself. I then awakened.

This dream, which has also served as a kind of touchstone during the research process, seems to have been a depiction of falling into the unknown with the only option being to surrender to my fate and remain present. Conducting research with soul in mind is in many ways the experience of falling into the unknown, being drawn to one's conclusion in such a way that demands complete submission.

It is its own form of initiation, complete with the danger of being undone in the process.

Another dream, which occurred much later in the course of the study, depicts a significant turning point in this transformative process. As mentioned, during much of the research process my experience was characterized by confusion, the feeling of being dumb, or unable to speak, and unable to be heard. This caused a great deal of anxiety and distress along the way. Therefore, when this dream occurred it was as if I had been visited by someone from beyond the veil, someone who had a larger field of vision than me and who could offer me encouragement and relief from the distress. I came to think of this dream as The Visitation.

> I had such tremendous relief when I had the dream, or the visitation, I should say, from the woman from the "other side." That's the best way I know to describe where it seemed she came from. She seemed to come from beyond the veil. I was so relieved and grateful to know that I'm not crazy, that there is a "beyond" and that I'm not alone. As I stepped out of the shower and was drying myself off, she told me that I would be getting pregnant. I was full of grief and my heart easily experienced the full sadness within me. It was a release to cry and know that she knew of my struggles with the question of motherhood and knew of my pain. She was an ally, someone on my side, with me, looking out for me. She made it sound like this was just a matter of course and it would happen. As I cried and my heart released the grief within it, I asked her if she knew how old I am. She said yes, she knew and that was why we needed to get on with it. This is all I really remember about the dream but as I awakened from it, a lyric from the Paul McCartney song "Let 'em in" was in my head. ("Someone's knocking at the door, somebody's ringing the bell.") Only the "Let 'em in" part was playing in my head upon waking. In the dream, I had the feeling, one that I've had maybe a few other times, where it doesn't seem like a dream but more like contact with the reality beyond the veil. It seemed very real and very clear. (Author's log book, July 14, 2011)

This dream was truly a gift of the research process in that the release of grief was profound and real. Inherent in the topic of this study about the child is the mother-child relationship. Although the dream clearly was not about actual pregnancy and childbirth, the research process is its own form of birthing process which, in this case, entails tending to the wounds of childhood and the mother-child relationship within myself. Receiving this visitation was the experience of being deeply known and understood, which is an incredibly healing experience and of course much of what the psychotherapy process is about. In this dream, the woman who visited me was an older woman, a motherly figure, tending to me as adult child about my own childbearing. As a counterpart and complement to The Dream of the Wild Child, this dream offered a release of the grief from the failings of motherhood and my failings as a mother. It was like cleaning the slate for new beginnings.

In working with this figure in the dream afterward, or engaging the "others" in the work, I conducted a transference dialogue.

> *Colette, fear not and don't worry. This takes your energy from where it needs to be. Stay in touch within your heart. Stay in tune and attuned. This will guide you out of the morass you feel yourself in. In working out of it, that is your purpose. Stay with it. Do not give up and do not question the process you are in. Know what you know.*

How do I make sense of the review of the literature I've been working on? There is so much confusion and chaos in my mind about this.

> *That is the state of the child. Confused, in chaos. This work will help align the child with her purpose. The child is within you.*

Who is this work for? Who do I serve in doing this work?

> *We all work for the same purpose. That is to unify and rectify our passion.*

How should I make sense of the work I have so far?

*Keep going. We are working on you and it is coming together. Don't try so hard. The ideas will begin to come to you more fluidly and you will begin to write them. . . . We are here to guide you. We are here to help you. The work is important to us as well. You committed to this work long ago. It is for healing and not just you. This began long ago.*

*Listen.*
*Listen inside. That is where we speak. There is much, it is vast within you. The doorway to the universe is within you. (Author's log book, July 14, 2011)*

A final dream marking the collaboration between the conscious and unconscious in the researcher and a demonstration of the transformative process occurred over a year later. This dream, "Cleansing the Divine," occurred on September 18, 2012. From the log book:

I was with a small group of people who were moving around with Jesus in a private, but regal or sacred place. I was behind Jesus so I did not see his face. The other people in the group were attending to him, I was an observer. We were moving about in this space. I was awestruck. It seemed sacred, to be in this place with him and them. At one point, Jesus was in something like a baptismal font and one of the people tending him was washing or anointing his back. He was in the water up to his waist and his back was broad. The washing was slow, soothing. I heard no sounds of water drops but it was clear the cleansing was happening. I was honored to be there and to witness this scene. (Author's log book, September 18, 2012)

The religious practice of baptism or cleansing as a release of sin and impurity intends to bring one into greater alignment with the divine, to atone, or bring together as one. Another purpose is to sanctify. What would the purpose of cleansing, purifying, or sanctifying Jesus be in this dream? What is the significance of my witnessing this ritual? Clearly, this was a numinous dream, with its sacred tone, my own experience of awe and the sense of it being a great honor to witness the scene. Although I did not know until the day after the dream occurred, this was the day *The New York Times* reported that biblical scholar Karen King had translated an ancient fragment of papyrus indicating that Jesus may have been married to Mary Magdelene (Goodstein, 2012). Was there any connection between this dream and the story in *The New York Times*?

In Jungian terms, the *coniunctio* is a conjoining of opposites, the sacred marriage between masculine and feminine, the divine and the human, heaven and earth. It is sometimes represented as a king bathing. Perhaps cleansing the divine signifies greater attunement between the divine and the human in that a marriage of the masculine and feminine within the religious context would be a more balanced integration of the transcendent and the immanent. With Jesus as transcendent and Mary as immanent, this recalls the interpermeating pyramids in which the sphera aequalatis is at the intersection between the two but cannot exist without either one of them and only exists in the interpenetration or in the tension between the opposites.

Without the *New York Times* article, how does this dream mark a final stage of the transformational process of research with soul in mind? As part of a series of dreams, this dream depicts my own experience of "knowing" the divine by being present to the bathing of Jesus. Again, the image of a king bathing, in the "language" of alchemy represents the coniunctio—the interpenetration of conscious and unconscious.

As products of the unconscious, these dreams depict both the engagement of the researcher with the work as well as an individuation process at work in the researcher. The individuation process as Jung defined it, is a psychological growth process in which there is a greater integration of the personal self and transpersonal Self. It is essentially a spiritual process. As De Laszlo (1990) stated in the introduction to *The Basic Writings of C. G. Jung*, "the individuation process can be said to lie at the core of all spiritual experience, since it is coequal with a creative transformation of the inner person, and hence reflects the archetypal experience of an inner rebirth" (p. xxxiii). The dream of Cleansing the Divine, as an archetypal representation of the coniunctio, may be seen as the outcome of the inner rebirth and the culmination of the "pregnancy" foretold in the dream of The Visitation.

Conducting research with soul in mind using the alchemical hermeneutic method transforms the hermeneutic circle into a spiral through deep engagement of the researcher with the work. Rather than attempting objectivity through separation of the researcher and the research topic, one's own subjectivity is used as a means of penetrating the deeper levels of meaning that paradoxically provide perhaps even greater objectivity on the topic than otherwise possible. The greater objectivity comes in acknowledging that the researcher and the work are both always subject to unconscious influence, and in acknowledging the transference field between the researcher and the work. In that the unconscious has been directly acknowledged and engaged by the researcher, the research is cleaner, more conscious, and the work itself may be heard more clearly, more purely, more "objectively."

This leads me to an articulation of theory in response to the research questions posed at the start of this study: How does spirituality influence a child's development of a sense of self and how is this mediated by a relationship with nature? What are the relationships between sense of self, spirituality and the natural world?

*Chapter Eight*

# Children's Spirituality, Sense of Self, and the Natural World: A Threefold Interpermeation

There is no such thing as a human being.

The context for this study widens beyond the question of development itself and beyond the question of how the developmental process affects the individual child; the context of this study postulates an inherent integration of spirituality and psychology to begin with, and poses questions addressing a larger whole—that of the human being and the earth. As a theoretical dissertation, the objective has been to investigate the interrelationships between self, spirituality, and the natural world in children, thus explorations into these relationships have defined the quest. As a theory-building endeavor, the aim has been neither to specifically address clinical issues, nor to address only developmental process, but to ensoul the work of both of these with a new perspective that ultimately contributes to them both.

The following observations, interpretations, and proposals for theory are my own summation and responses to the research question: how does spirituality contribute to the child's development of a sense of self and how does a relationship with the natural world play a part in this interaction? Taking an imaginal approach to this study, I have intentionally used my *self* as a venue into the realms to be explored, and I have attempted to include contributions from the unconscious along the way. My tentative conclusions therefore result from the alchemical hermeneutic method of attending to the world of soul, the "domain of reality between the domains of matter and mind" (Romanyshyn, 2007, p. 81).

For the purpose of clarity, I have generally made declarative statements in my proposals for theory. These statements are made, however, with the acknowledgment that in using the hermeneutic method, the work is never done, there is always something left unsaid. Further, I have attempted to be a "servant" (Palmer, 1969, p. 208) of the work, and I have attempted to be open to a new "vision of reality" (p. 9). What follows is a result of this whole process; it is the new vision of reality that became clear to me during the course of this study.

## Self-Reflective Consciousness and Unconscious Myths at Work

After contemplating the literature on self and sense of self development from the fields of developmental psychology, psychoanalytic self psychology and analytical psychology, it became clear that the phenomenological experience of oneself as a person in the world, coupled with self-reflective consciousness, is what leads to the attempts by scholars and theorists to conceptualize what the self is and how it develops. The ability to self-reflect is also what leads us to ponder the questions of who and what I am, who and what are the people around me, and what do I (or we) make of this experience of living. Further, this capacity is at the heart of spiritual inquiry.

**The myth of the isolated mind.** In making use of self-reflective consciousness, it is possible to see ourselves as subjects looking out on a field of objects. Inherent in this perspective is the notion that as an individual, I am separated from other people and the world around me. If I am separated from other people around me, I can probably find a way to get past my own subjectivity to a theoretical "place" or perspective where objectivity is possible. I then believe I can take myself out of the equation and see how objects interact with one another, without myself in the middle. Stolorow and Atwood (1994) helped us see that a Cartesian-flavored myth unconsciously organizing our experience has been at work in these ponderings—that of the myth of the isolated mind.

Our self-reflective consciousness inherently allows for this type of myth to operate. In fact, this was the basis of Descartes' statement, *I think therefore I am,* and is where the myth of the isolated mind gained standing as a common sense, albeit *unconscious,* perspective (Stolorow & Atwood, 1992). Again, if our minds are separate or isolated from one another, then each of us is separate from others. (Of course, on one level, this is clearly true, and it must be stated that disregard for individuality is the basis of significant psychopathology; however, on another level or from a spiritual perspective, this is not necessarily true. The purpose of this study is, once again, to explore the relation between self and spirituality while drawing attention to the inherent integration of spirituality and psychology. As such, statements that seem to contradict one another, such as "clearly we are separate but we are one" must make their way into the conclusions of the study.)

**The myth of the mind-body separation.** The myth of the isolated mind is closely correlated with another myth—that of the mind-body separation. If I am the subject looking out on other objects and I recognize this, then I can also see myself as an object. This means I can differentiate between my thoughts and my physical existence, which in turn means that my thoughts can be disembodied—could exist outside of me. This would mean that the mind and the body are not one. The self and the body are not one. This is, again, the dualistic paradigm that not only impacts our psychological theories and beliefs but also our spiritual perspective and relationship with the Self or the divine.

We can, however, reorient the nature of the ponderings in self-reflection when the myth of an isolated mind has been debunked. The phenomenological experience of being a person in the world within an intersubjective context in which there is no such thing as a truly isolated mind, results in the recognition that ultimately, all of us are co-creating our experiences together, as a collective. This is, of course, a theoretical extrapolation of the overturning of the myth of the isolated mind but it is useful in gaining new perspective on ourselves as a collective, in the world. From this perspective, political antagonism in this country is no longer a matter of whether one party is right and another is wrong, but a question of co-creation and co-regulation. From this perspective we might ask questions such as, how am I contributing to the political divisiveness that has taken place in this election year? Am I, as an individual (or perhaps as a news source, political party, or company) working to regulate myself within this political divisiveness or am I somehow contributing to the bi-polarity that seems to be manifesting in the collective American psyche? Or, questions about how we contribute to the destruction of the natural world might become relevant, even for those who consider themselves to be operating with mindfulness of the abuse of the natural world. The starting place for ponderings about ourselves and the world is different when the dualistic paradigm is no longer patterning our thoughts and experiences.

**The myth of the separation between human beings and the earth.** With acknowledgment of the myths of the isolated mind and the mind-body split, we have a new perspective in exploring questions about the relationship between human beings and Earth. If we draw parallels and make connections between the intersubjective, human to human context and the larger context of human beings and the natural world, we have a new way to consider the greater implications of these myths. No longer does the myth of the mind-body split apply only to the relation between the human body and the human mind, it also applies to human beings and the earth; the separation between mind and body parallels the myth of the separation of the human being and the earth. When we see ourselves as separate from the natural world, this is a reverberation of both the myth of the isolated mind and that of the mind-body split.

**There is no such thing as a human being.** When we set aside these myths, however, we may consider the notion that human beings, as self-reflective, conscious beings, are the consciousness of the earth, or the "earth mind" of the "earth body." This is what Berry (2006) referred to in recognizing human thought as its own "sphere" in *earth* functioning: that of the noosphere. Rather than human beings and the earth being separate from one another, perhaps there is a greater integration between them, wherein human beings and the earth are one. This would parallel the greater integration between the mind and body that comes when we denounce the Cartesian dualism that sets up the ghost-in-the-machine type of mind/body split pervading Western thought. With these myths revealed, we can then see how, truly, not only is there no such thing as an infant, as Winnecott stated, but there is no such thing as a human being without the context of other human beings and the world around us. In this sense, all of us are "going on being," both individually and collectively.

These are the unconscious "myths" or false collective beliefs brought into my own awareness during the research process. In conjunction with the literature reviewed, the alchemical hermeneutic method used during the research process brought into awareness the fallacy of these beliefs or assumptions and revealed a new perspective on the central questions of this study. From this new perspective, I have drawn further theoretical conclusions about the interrelation between self, spirituality and the natural world, which follow.

## Sense of Self Development Occurs in the Greater Context of the Human-Earth Relationship

There has been a progression over time in the psychological literature of greater and greater acknowledgement of the two-way impact of the relationship between a baby and her mother or primary caregiver. Not only is the infant greatly affected by the exchanges with the mother, the mother is also affected by the exchanges with the infant. In addition, not only conscious exchanges but also unconscious exchanges greatly affect the developing sense of self. Mother's unconscious orientation clearly has great impact on her interactions with her baby. This is particularly important if we consider that the unconscious extends from the personal level to the deeper, collective levels of the psyche, including the natural world, per the Jungian view of the unconscious.

Implicit in the mother's interactions with the infant then, are both her conscious attitudes and experiences within the natural world, and her unconscious attitudes, as well as her unconscious embeddedness within the natural world. This must play a part in the context of that relationship between the infant and the mother or caregiver, even if this occurs on a very subtle level. Thus, looking at the development of the self in infancy and beyond, it seems important to acknowledge that if the imagination of the parents about the infant affects the infant's growing sense of self, then there would be no limitation on the breadth of the imagination in the adult and either a sense of the embeddedness within the natural world is implicitly communicated, or a sense of disconnection or dissociation from the natural world would also be communicated. This disconnection or dissociation might come from the individual mother directly or, as she is part of a human collective, this dissociation might come from a level of the collective unconscious that undergirds human society. This acknowledgment is important not only in the discussion of self and sense of self development but as a point of integration with the questions of spirituality as well as the human-nature relationship. Unconscious contributions and the principle of reciprocity exist in the relationships in and between each of the three aspects of this study—self, spirituality, and the natural world.

**Attachment and other non-verbal exchanges in the mother-infant context.** The domain of intersubjective relatedness exists outside of conscious awareness and therefore without being rendered verbally, until it is brought into awareness and symbolized with language. As discussed in the findings on self and sense of self development, much of the context co-created by mother and infant entails nonverbal attunements and exchanges between subjects. The quality of attachment, though not *directly* causally related to specific outcomes, is nonetheless critical in the development of a sense of self.

**The psychosomatic unity of the self and bodily memory.** In this development, the psychological is continuous with the physiological although once again self-reflective consciousness and Cartesian dualism lead us to "see" these as separate. Although there is clearly differentiation between the physiological and the psychological, ultimately there is a unity of phenomenological experience. In other words, the human being is a psychosomatic unity. As a psychosomatic unity, the child retains on some level a bodily "memory" of attachment and relational experiences (as well as other experiences) which is interwoven in the developing sense of self. Recent neuropsychological research as well as research on alternative forms of psychotherapy techniques such as EMDR[1] address the issue of bodily memory or patterning of experiences.

**Nonverbal attunements and exchanges between human beings and the natural world.** With this acknowledgement and the incorporation of findings on the human-nature connection, I am postulating that there also exists a range of nonverbal attunements and exchanges between human beings, especially children, and the natural

---

[1] Eye Movement Desensitization and Reprocessing

world which are also interwoven with the child's developing sense of self. When we consider ourselves as subjects in relationship with the subjects of the natural world, we are recognizing that beyond self-reflective consciousness there exist other possibilities for subjectivity in the natural world. Berry (2006) exhorts us to shift our perspective from seeing the natural world as a collection of objects to experiencing ourselves in the world within a communion of subjects. From this perspective, the context of intersubjective relatedness then broadens beyond human to human interaction and becomes inclusive of human to natural world interaction.

Just as our understanding of the exchange between the mother and child has evolved, our perspective on the natural world might evolve in appreciation of the greater richness of the context co-created between us. We might expand the scope of our exploration to wonder about the actual relationship between ourselves as human beings and the natural world, rather than unconsciously dismissing such considerations due to the expectation that relationships only happen in conscious-mind to conscious-mind engagements.

My work with the transference dialogues directly contributed to this shift in perspective. The statement "when there is abuse, all are wounded" made it clear that there is no psychological differentiation between wounding of the person or wounding of the earth. This is only clear when it is recognized that human beings and the earth are one.

**The natural world as Selfobject.** As discussed in the findings on sense of self development, one of the "directions" for growth is in the self-Self relationship, with parents serving as conduits for Selfobject experiences. In other words, the infant or child engages with the transpersonal Self via interactions with the parent. Based on my findings in this study, I suggest that the natural world may also serve as a Selfobject for the child, allowing for Selfobject experiences to take place in engagements with the natural world. Selfobject experiences as "affect-laden, enhanced self-states" (Lichtenberg, 2001, p. 134) clearly take place with regularity in the natural world, as evidenced in the collected stories of Robinson (1983) and others. When there is subject-to-subject engagement between the child and the natural world, without the expectation of entirely language-based interaction as the means of engagement, the child has the opportunity for

Selfobject experiences which contribute to the sense of self. Another way of stating this is that these Selfobject experiences strengthen the connection between the self and the transpersonal Self within the child. With a stronger sense of spiritual connection to the transpersonal Self, the child's sense of self is enhanced.

**Greater contact with the natural world leads to its integration in the sense of self.** The bodily "memory" of experiences, particularly experiences in the natural world, takes on greater significance when we consider once again the collective levels of the unconscious. With the human being as a psychosomatic unity, and an ongoing exchange between conscious and unconscious levels of the psyche at work, the more physical separation experienced in relation with the natural world, the greater the impact on the individual sense of self and in turn, the greater the impact on collective consciousness. On the other hand, the greater the experience of physical, psychological, and spiritual connection with the natural world, the more the sense of self is interwoven with the experience of the earth-human unity and the reciprocal human-earth relationship. Thus a three-way reciprocal exchange occurs between sense of self, spirituality, and the natural world with each contributing to the other.

**The use of metaphor in understanding and making meaning of the human-earth relationship.** The significance of the mother-infant context to the question of the inter-relatedness of self, spirituality and the natural world becomes more clear when we make use of our ability and propensity to use metaphor to understand and make meaning of our existence as human beings. Metaphoric thinking based on the natural world helps us as human beings penetrate a deeper meaning to human life. Metaphoric thinking based on human relationships might also help penetrate a deeper meaning to the human-earth relationship. (The metaphors themselves are also a reflection of our interrelationship with the natural world, as well as our increasing disconnection from it coinciding with the greater and greater use of electronics. Note how often metaphors are now based on technology as opposed to the natural world and how computing terminology makes its way into our language and dialogue. This is a point I will return to in the Discussion chapter as it addresses a point made in the statement of a need for research on this topic.)

If we draw parallels between the mother-infant context with its significance in the development of a sense of self, to the human-nature connection, it becomes easier to see that the context of our being as members of the natural world is interwoven with the sense of self, whether this is conscious or not. However, given that we now see what happens when we live out the fallacy of the myth of our separation from the natural world in the readily apparent worldwide environmental destruction and devastation, it is clear that our interdependence and entirely embedded relationship with the natural world can no longer remain a disprovable hypothesis but instead must be brought to conscious awareness as an inevitable (or perhaps wondrous) fact of life.

If asked, I speculate that most people would agree that logically there is no way to live separated from the natural world because, clearly, we are 100% dependent on it. Nonetheless, in many, many ways, we do live *as though* we are separate from the natural world, seemingly resenting our dependence on it, hating the unpredictability and discomforts that being a part of the natural world sometimes brings. Consider how often we begrudge the rain, the cold, or the snow when it inconveniences us, brings discomfort, or damages our man-made structures. In the industrialized world a significant portion of our current existence on the planet has to do with denying our dependence on the natural world and insulating ourselves from the reality of the variability of weather, climate, and terrain, as well as the reality of our dependence on natural resources to enable our current mode of existence. This is what Stolorow and Atwood (1994) meant by their statement that the myth of the isolated mind is, in part, a disavowel of human vulnerabilities in and cycles of biological existence" ("Alienation from Nature," para. 1).

**Examples of the human sense of disconnection from the natural world.** Human beings create worlds within worlds that are pure encapsulations of the idea that we can exist without the natural world interfering with us. For example, The Venetian hotel in Las Vegas is a world within a world, complete with a false canal and Hollywood set-like "skies" that go dimmer as the "sun" goes down. In this "world," human beings are not subject to the variability of the natural world. The Venetian, however, is a replica of a city which in its own right was already a created world. I find it fascinating to know that Venice itself is actually built on many, many timber piles harvested from the forests of Croatia and Slovenia and driven deep into the bed of the Venetian Lagoon. This is a stunning example of how human beings demonstrate our "dominion" over the earth and her resources. Venice's rich culture and history, as well as the improbable fact of its existence— like a magical kingdom on the sea, is enchanting and even beguiling to us as a marvel of human ingenuity and creativity. Although for thousands of years we have exercised dominion over the earth with relatively little repercussion for the entirety of the planet, it is now apparent that with the use of machinery and technology, our dominion has become threatening to the survival of the planet or at least to the survival of untold numbers of living species, not the least of which might be our own. This, again, is a depiction of how the sense of self is interwoven with the natural world and how the degree of connection or disconnection is made manifest in how we live our lives and in the structures, towns, and cities we build.

In the example of The Venetian hotel in Las Vegas, the disconnection from the natural world and the denial of our dependence on the natural world are made manifest in the re-creation of an experience which was itself already a demonstration of our ability to dominate our natural surroundings. During Venice's construction over 1000 years ago, it is clear that a greater integration between human beings and the natural world existed, if for no other reason than the absence of industrial machinery and electronic technology. The experience of the "real" Venice still involves the natural world, which is part of its appeal and wonder, but the Venetian Hotel is a step further removed, cutting out the natural world altogether and recreating it such that human beings are in control of all aspects of the environment.

Both the myth of the isolated mind and the dualistic paradigm contribute to a sense that the self exists separate from the natural world. All scholarly literature on self and sense of self development has been written by human beings who, by necessity, are embodied beings. Although this seems obvious, it is helpful to be reminded when considering the capacity for self-reflective awareness that develops in the course of infancy and childhood. This capacity of the mind to reflect back on itself and to imagine itself as separate from others or to give the experience of looking out from an interior space, is also the starting point for dissociation from the physical body as well as dissociation from the natural world. In addition, however, it is the starting point for the awareness of the psychosomatic unity of the self, as well as the awareness of the impossibility of human life as separate from the natural world. Although we can imagine that we are distinct and separate from the natural world, which translates into an unconscious belief that we could somehow leave it or do without it, this is clearly impossible, just as it is impossible for the self to exist without a body. The self is by necessity a psychosomatic unity. There is no self to consider unless one is considering it within the body. There is not even a divine Self to consider for that too, occurs from within a body. Nonetheless, both the myth of the isolated mind and the myth of the mind/body split persist and find their way into everyday life.

To continue with the example of Venice, there is now a manifestation of our further dissociation and disconnection from the natural world in the "virtual" world and an example of the persistence of the mind/body split. One can have a "virtual" experience of Venice on "Second Life," which is an online virtual world, experienced only in the minds of the people who participate via a virtual self or what they call an "avatar." As advertised on the *Second Life* website,

> few things are more amore-riffic than a gondola ride through the canals at sunset with your avatar beloved. It's fitting that you can take a stroll through the Venetian streets, check out the carnival masks—and yes, ride the gondolas—in this homage to Italian culture. Turn down the lights with your graphics settings at Ultra for candlelight-dinner-worthy results. (SOphia Inkpen, 2012)

An "avatar" in computing, is "the graphical that is used to represent a real person in a cyberspace or three-dimensional system" (Collin, S. 2010). It is no coincidence that this term originated in Hinduism, in which context it has spiritual meaning. In Hinduism, an avatar is basically the incarnation or embodiment of a divine being. In computing, an avatar is the disembodiment of the self. This is a very clear, concrete illustration of the myth of the mind/body split and its progression over time in our culture. It is an unconscious reflection of this myth; you can take the person out of the body to live in a virtual world. As we become further and further disconnected from the natural world and more and more embedded in the world of electronics, our sense of self is literally being interwoven with the world(s) in which we engage.

**Human beings are 100% interdependent with the natural world.** There are plenty of examples of both the disconnection from the natural world, evidence of the unconscious hatred of the natural world, and the myth of the mind/body split. Venice, The Venetian hotel, and the online Venice in Second Life simply depict one concrete example of this. The counterpart, however, to the disconnection and dissociation from the natural world, is the recognition that human beings are 100% *inter*dependent with the natural world, and that the sense of self develops within the context of that relationship, no matter the quality of the relationship. Just as the infant's sense of self develops within the context of the relationship with the mother, no matter the quality of that relationship, so the sense of self of human beings develops within the context of our relationship with the natural world. When this is recognized, the relationship between human beings and the planet, and particularly between children and the natural world can be nurtured and "allowed" to have their natural interplay.

**Interpermeating relationships between self, spirituality and the natural world.** The spiritual life of the child depends upon this connection, and the sense of self of the child is in turn deeply affected by the spiritual nature of the child's existence. From a purely spatial perspective, it is impossible to understand the interrelationship between self, spirituality, and the natural world, because it is impossible for one thing to be in another while that other is in the first. From a spiritual perspective, however, and with the use of the archetype of the interpenetrating pyramids as discussed in the previous chapter, (or what I now see as the Eastern counterpart to this archetype—the yin yang symbol) it is comprehensible to see that the relationships between self, spirituality, and the natural world are "interpermeating" (W. Adams, 1999) with each deeply affecting the other. The child's sense of self then, is directly impacted by both the relationship with the natural world, and by her spiritual nature. Spirituality, as an "axis" or as a dimension of experience connecting the self with Self, the self with the natural world, and the Self with the natural world, is both that which makes it possible for the child to have a sense of transcendence and connection to something greater than himself, and at the same time, is that which, within the child, allows for a sense of meaning, allows faith to develop, and is that intangible quality that leads to wonder, wondering, wisdom, mystery and awareness sensing, and the experience of being connected to something greater than oneself.

**Spirituality, spiritual experiences, and the sense of self.** When a child has spiritual experiences, or when the spiritual nature of the child is nurtured in experience, the axis between the self and the transpersonal Self is strengthened and potentiates further spiritual growth. Clearly, not all spiritual growth occurs as the result of what we might consider "positive" spiritual experiences; often spiritual growth occurs in the aftermath of hardship or during intense experiences requiring the use of spiritual faculties such as faith, morality, and compassion. However, the spiritual experiences and spiritual growth of the child contribute, as they occur, to the child's developing sense of self. This is part of the integrating function of spirituality.

**The spiritual life of the child is nurtured in communion with the natural world.** As discussed, that which makes us most fully human is our spiritual nature. One of the ways this nature must be cultivated is in our relationship with the natural world. A wordless communication or communion with the natural world nurtures the spirit of the child because of the context co-created between them. Similar to the relationship between an infant and a mother or primary caregiver, in which there are multiple levels of exchange and co-participation, there is a spiritual form of the "string resonance" mentioned earlier in regard to the unconscious attunements between the mother and infant. In other words, the child's physical presence in the natural world allows for a resonance and connection with plants, trees, animals, and the elements that nurtures the spirit of the child and in turn the child's sense of self. Some of this resonance and attunement comes from perceptual experience—sights, sounds, smells, tastes, and touch— whereas some of it occurs outside of awareness and is completely unconscious. As in the relationship between the mother and infant, in which the domain of intersubjective relating includes unconscious, unknown, or unrecognized means of exchange, so in the human–earth relationship, the resonance that occurs results in part from unconscious, unknown, or unrecognized means of exchange.

*Gratitude as a spiritual faculty.* The resonance, communion, and attunements between the child and the natural world contribute to the spiritual life of the child by nurturing and cultivating spiritual capacities and faculties. Especially when the child's experience is mediated by an attuned and earth-connected adult (Carson, 1998), the child's sense of wonder and sense of appreciation can be cultivated. Wonder and wondering open the way for contemplation of the mysteries of life, which is one of the most distinctly human spiritual capacities. Appreciation, likewise, is a distinctly human capacity closely related to what I would call the spiritual "faculty" of gratitude. Gratitude, as a faculty, allows an inner sense of the self giving way or opening in an acknowledgement of receiving from another or appreciation of another. It is both a faculty that makes this possible, and an emotional state. When one is in a state of gratitude, one recognizes and appreciates what one has received. Between people, this might be anything from an act of service to a compliment, and between children and the natural world this might be the appreciation of beauty, gentleness, fierceness, complexity, or gratitude for a source of food, animal companionship, or emotional comfort. When one has a sense of gratitude either to other people or to the natural world, the inner sense of the self giving way or opening sets the stage for a sense of transpersonal connection. One has a sense of belonging and there is meaning in that sense, even if this is not completely conscious while it is happening. This opening or giving way of the self might also be related to experiences of transcendence in that the inner state of the child is "primed" or prepared for the experience of transcendence by repeated experiences of appreciation and gratitude. The affect-laden, enhanced self states discussed by Lichtenberg (2001) as contributing to the developing sense of self might be seen from this perspective. What we consider spiritual attributes, capacities, or faculties are their own *spiritual* motivational system, propelling the child forward in fulfillment of her own potential, in making meaning of her life and the world around her, and ultimately in preparing her to make her own contribution to the whole. Therefore, the same faculties nurtured in connecting with the natural world are spiritual faculties contributing to the child's growing sense of self.

*Additional spiritual faculties.* In addition to the spiritual capacities already discussed, as well as the faculty of gratitude, I would argue, first of all, that there are additional spiritual faculties: faith and compassion, and secondly, that these faculties are nurtured in the child in the early context of the infant-mother/primary caregiver relationship and during experiences of communing with the natural world.

Beginning during the emergence of the early senses of self and attachment to the mother, the groundwork is laid for all of these spiritual faculties to find their own emergence. Gratitude and faith stem from that trusting bond between mother and infant. The experience of gratitude occurs in a relational context. Likewise, faith develops in relational context, giving the child a sense of trusting connection to something greater than the self. Compassion, stemming from the empathic connection between mother and infant, also serves the child to have a spiritual connection to other people and the natural world. Thus the mother-infant bond, embedded within the human-nature relationship, sets the stage for the cultivation of spiritual faculties throughout life.

These spiritual faculties may be enhanced in the child during engagement and communion with the natural world. Each of these faculties—gratitude, faith, and compassion, is used in the engagement and communion with the natural world. They are the means of connection with the natural world and are therefore enhanced when a sense of connection occurs. The spiritual faculties address the fundamental interdependence and connectedness of human beings and all other animate and inanimate life forms on the planet. In other words, they are all relationship or *context*-furthering faculties.

*Gratitude.* Gratitude, as the opening and giving way of the self, allows openness to all of the transcendent experiences people have described themselves as having in the natural world. Even if a person is not particularly feeling a sense of gratitude in the moment, gratitude is like the gateway experience to greater spiritual connection to the natural world. Without the sense of the self giving way and opening to receive, having a sense of connection is limited to the perceptual or cognitive, which means there is not an affective sense of connection.

*Faith.* Faith, as a way of knowing and being in the world, based on early and ongoing relational life experiences, is also nurtured in the relational context of the human being and the earth. When the child has experiences of communing with the natural world, wrote Fowler (1981), the child's imagination about the "ultimate environment" (p. 33), is infused with these experiences. As Fowler stated, faith "composes a felt image of an ultimate environment" (p. 33). Therefore, experiences in the natural world, particularly those mediated by reverent adults, contribute to this felt image within the child and shape the child's faith. The immanence of the transpersonal Self both within the child and within the natural world may be experienced when there are opportunities to be in the natural world in a way that is engaging to the child.

*Compassion.* Compassion is a loosening of the boundary that seemingly separates one from others. Compassion as a spiritual faculty stems from the ability to make empathic connections, once again beginning with early life experiences. It is a form of love and the heart of the Golden Rule. Compassion allows one to see what spiritual teachers have seen when they counsel us to do unto others as you would have done unto yourself. As an emotional experience, it involves more than the cognitive recognition of the ethical value of following the Golden Rule; it includes the empathic connection allowing the sense of a shared feeling to be a guide.

When children are in the natural world, the resonant context facilitates a sense of connection, empathy, and compassion toward the world around them. Being in the natural world, looking closely at the fine detail of an insect or a flower, being still and observant in order to catch a glimpse of a woodland creature, these activities with the accompanying state of being prepare the child for making compassionate connections. Particularly with animals, the potential for developing compassion within children through their engagement with the animals is great. Once again, experiences mediated by guiding adults are important and contribute both to the child's spiritual development as well as to the adult's.

## Shifting Perspective on the Relationship Between Human Beings and the Earth

If we look at human beings as separate from the earth and superior to all other existence, then human concerns become all important. In this paradigm our focus is on how human beings get along with one another, how well they function in their own lives, whether they live a meaningful life or not, and whether there is pathology that interrupts functioning, relationships, and existential concerns. From this perspective, spending time in the natural world might be considered as a way to ameliorate psychological maladies but this is simply part of the role of the natural world as backdrop for the drama of the human being. If, however, we do not buy into the myth of the isolated mind or the myth of the mind/body split which, together, translate into the myth of the separation between human beings and the earth, and instead, we take into consideration the interrelationships between human beings and the earth, then our perspective on self and consciousness necessarily shifts.

The question of the nature of consciousness is an enormous realm of study and beyond the scope of the current study to explore in any depth. However, my fidelity to the alchemical hermeutic method used in this study dictates that the following facet of my proposal for theory must be laid out in order for the entirety of the new "vision of reality" (Palmer, 1969, p. 9) to be depicted.

**The role of consciousness and the self in the greater context of the human-earth relationship.** Under the myth of the all-important isolated mind, in general, consciousness serves the human being. It serves in the growth of the self, it serves one in relationships and in living a meaningful life. Although these will remain important to us no matter the shift in perspective we might make, it is worthwhile to consider the role of the self and consciousness in the larger context of the human-earth relationship.

The review of literature on the human-nature connection made it clear that more and more psychologists are bringing awareness to our relationship with the earth. Perhaps the relatively recent phenomenon of environmental destruction significant enough to bring about climate change has ushered in a heightened awareness of the importance of our relationship with the natural world. More and more people seem to realize we have an impact not just on our immediate surroundings but on much larger or even global natural systems such as weather patterns, pollination, clean water, and countless other natural systems that, in turn, have a direct impact on human life.

As we experience the effects of our own actions as a species on the world around us, we learn more about our place in the world. We can now see, with the help of way-showers like Jung, Berry, Rozsak, Macy, and many others, that human beings have a different relationship with the earth than what we might have understood not long ago. Rather than human beings having dominion over the earth and exploiting the earth for what we think is our own evolution and advancement, we now begin to see that we might actually have a supporting role in someone else's story. That story would be the story of Earth. Consciousness, rather than an achievement that we can claim as our own, might actually be a part of a greater evolutionary process. If this is the case, as human beings we are no longer the reigning intelligence, but are perhaps in the *service of* intelligence and consciousness. To illustrate this point, a nature-based analogy might be helpful.

When the very first oxygen producing microorganisms began breathing out oxygen molecules in the first stages of the evolution of an atmosphere around this planet billions of years ago, no doubt there was *not* a sense of ownership of this miraculous new process that had been discovered by these micro-organisms—the humble and enduring blue-green algae. With the discovery of this process of photosynthesis wherein an organism essentially feeds itself by way of the sun and emits oxygen as a by-product, an entirely new sphere of life evolved on the planet: the atmosphere, that relatively thin, oxygen-rich layer of gases surrounding our planet which happens to be essential to life on Earth.

Fast forward to the evolution of the noosphere: the sphere of human thought. We can ask, did human beings invent consciousness? Is consciousness ours? Does it belong to us? That is clearly not the case although just as we live *as if* we can be separate from the natural world, we live *as if* human beings are the inventors of consciousness. Unconsciously, there is the idea that because we make use of it in our lives, it belongs to us. Of course, on one level, we are each responsible for our own consciousness. On another level, we can ask whether consciousness is serving us or we are serving consciousness.

Ecology shows us that nothing on this planet is a closed system cut off from everything else. We know that when we pollute the air in the skies above Newark, New Jersey, the pollution does not remain in New Jersey. We know that our fresh water is part of a complex process involving an ever-circulating system interwoven with the entire planet. Any aspect of life on the planet must be considered in concert with the rest of the planet. In the context of this study, this observation begs the question: why would consciousness be any different? Why would consciousness be only a human achievement meant to serve human beings with disregard for the rest of the planet? Once again, the blue-green algae were the early *vehicles* for the production of oxygen in the atmosphere but that was only the beginning of a whole new chapter in the story of the evolution of the planet. Perhaps consciousness, since it has evolved within the context of the life of the planet, is a more integral part of the functioning of the earth—like air, like water, like life in general. From this perspective, we can see a vast new area of the unknown.

**The self as the *sphaera aequalatis*.** Returning to the interpenetrating pyramids, the archetypal contribution from the unconscious discussed in the previous chapter, the *sphaera aequalatis* is the center point between the two pyramids. It is in this centerpoint where the tension of the opposites is held together. As Robert Fludd described it, the sphaera aequalatis is the place between heaven and earth, between the divine and the human (Vickers, 1986). As an archetype, it seems to me to also be the world of soul between mind and matter or the sacred marriage between masculine and feminine. It is an archetype representing the overturning of the dualistic paradigm. In this respect, it represents a nondual vision of reality.

Within the context of the current study, this archetype helps to reveal a new perspective on the self in its role within the context of life as we know it. The self is in the sphaera aequalatis and it is where consciousness manifests itself. Consciousness, however, is not centered in cognition. Consciousness emerges in the realm of the heart where wisdom, intuition, and the other ways of knowing reveal spiritual meaning. During the day in which the reverie about the interpenetrating pyramids took place described in the previous chapter, the synthesizing moment came to me while I sat in preparation for yoga and gazed at the painting in front of me. The Star of David represents the heart chakra, the center chakra in the body. This chakra is also sometimes represented by the lotus, a symbol of spiritual enlightenment. It is in this place—in the heart of the human being—where the deepest sense of self and spiritual connection resides. This is the place where human consciousness as awareness and spiritual enlightnement emerges.

Like the blue-green algae were the vehicles for oxygen production, perhaps the self is the vehicle for consciousness. The self, at the centerpoint between the natural world and the spiritual or the divine, has its existence in that place of the tension between the opposites. It is where consciousness emerges, like the surf as it touches the shore, emerging from something the whole of which is much greater than we could possibly see as a whole.

Thus the human-nature relationship shifts in our consciousness when we take this meta-perspective. How spirituality contributes to the development of a sense of self becomes a question of how we repair the myths that stand in the way of seeing the oneness of human existence with all the rest. When we recognize the spiritual nature of children, we can see how important this is to the development of a sense of self. We can see how important it is, not just for the individual but for the greater good, that children have the opportunity to develop a sense of self connected to the earth. We can see how having the felt sense of connection to the earth nurtures the spiritual life of the child.

If we, as a collective of human beings, have a service to provide for the evolution of Earth, we certainly must learn to be conscious in attuned relationship with Earth. If we see ourselves as separate from the earth, rather than in relationship, we become more like an illness threatening the health of the planet than a function that serves moving forward in greater complexity and in, as yet, unknown directions. Who knows what forms of life or forms of consciousness are yet to evolve on this planet as a result of the heart-centered consciousness in human beings? What will be the next sphere to evolve out of the intermingling and cooperation of the geosphere, the hydrosphere, the biosphere, the atmosphere, and the most recent and miraculous noosphere? Surely each new sphere, like a new sense of self, must be experienced somewhere as a new kind of competence.

## Chapter Nine

# I Am You, You Are Me

We have subtle subconscious faculties we are not using. In addition to the limited analytic intellect is a vast realm of mind that includes psychic and extrasensory abilities; intuition; wisdom; a sense of unity; aesthetic, qualitative, and creative capacities; and image-forming and symbolic capacities. Though these faculties are many, we give them a single name with some justification because they are operating best when they are in concert. They comprise a mind, moreover, in spontaneous connection to the cosmic mind. This total mind we call "heart."

Helminski, 1992, p. 157

## Implications of the Methodology and the Findings of this Study for Clinical Psychology

Conducting research with soul in mind (Romanyshyn, 2007) is one way of recognizing the integration of the spiritual and the psychological in human life. Though using a strictly hermeneutic method in the foregoing study may have yielded shades of the same conclusions, my experience suggests that adding the alchemical hermeneutic method significantly transformed the outcome of this endeavor. Taking an imaginal approach, with its processes and method of making a place for the unconscious engagement of the researcher with the work, brought depth and dimensionality to the work in a surprisingly reliable way. This only became clear however, toward the end of the study. It was apparently only after a sufficient period of time in darkness and confusion that the fog of the unknown began to lift and the light of new awareness began to dawn. Thus the research process in many ways was a spiritual endeavor, working to hear from the unconscious, to hear what had been left unsaid in the research topic, and to hear, through my own wounding and the journey of the research process, what needed to be heard from my own soul. Only in deepening this personal sense of connection to the work was I able to hear the voice of the child, to make the shifts in perspective that led to the findings and outcome of this study.

This implies that conducting research in this way is both the means of personal growth and transformation as well as the means of penetrating a research topic with an ethic of service and responsibility. This kind of research requires and cultivates the full presence of the researcher in the research process. Presence then, takes center stage as the key player in this drama. Presence is that quality of transpersonal connection that sees the one in all and the all in one.

Using the imaginal approach to research and the alchemical hermeneutic method reliably served to widen the reach of the light of consciousness into the dark of the unconscious, or perhaps to bring the dark of the unconscious into the light of consciousness. Although reliable, it is not necessarily without its own peril, however. Like an initiation which tests the limits of the initiate and brings, at the very least, some measure of discomfort, or danger at most, doing research in this way will not conform to the structure of mechanistic or superficial exercises. In other words, there is no cheating the system or faking the results if one understakes to conduct research in this way.

This implies that with this method, clinical psychology has an effective, ethical means of conducting meaningful research that addresses the actual issues arising in our society today. Because the unconscious carries what has been left unsaid on the individual and collective levels, this means of penetrating the unconscious may serve as a counterbalance to the addiction to fact-based information that seems to have us running faster and faster after the truth and yet taking us further and further away from a grounded, connected way of living as a human community. Though, clearly, there are many fields of inquiry producing many potentially life-changing discoveries and innovations, just as clearly, the intensity of some of the global dysfunction continues to escalate. Doubtless, the silver bullet or the panacea for the ills of the earth does not exist; however, the prospect of becoming more fully human does hold some promise of greater balance amongst human beings and between human beings and our home planet, Earth. Thus engaging in psychological research in such a way that furthers one's own spiritual growth while also serving to tap into collective wounding seems a valuable aspect of becoming more fully human as a global community.

## Implications of This Study for Children

The implications of this study for children suggest that it is in our utmost interest to allow children greater opportunity to develop a sense of spiritual self in relationship with the earth. Children need time in the natural world to commune, reflect, and contemplate questions about themselves, their lives, and the world. They need opportunities to connect with the natural world in order for the spiritual self to emerge in the direction of human-earth unity. The natural world is for children the primary place to develop compassion, empathy, gratitude, and a sense of the sacred. Children need both time for unstructured play in the natural world as well as time with adults who mediate their experiences and help them cultivate a respectful relationship with the natural world. Adults too, need the opportunity for their own spiritual growth in engaging with children in this way. Both the child and the adult receive benefit when the child's spiritual growth and the connection to the natural world are valued and encouraged.

## Suggestions for Future Research

Future research designed to further investigate the proposals for theory stated in this study will aid in determining the validity of the study. In particular, interviews with children regarding their experience in the natural world would help bring clarity to the issue of the quality of experience in the natural world. For example, a study comparing the experiences of children in a traditional environmental education program and a program such as those offered at The Center for Education, Imagination and the Natural World would shed light on qualitative differences between programs and the impact of these difference on the children's experiences. In addition, differences in the role of the adult and differences in the opportunity to *commune* with the natural world versus *cognitive learning* about the natural world would help determine the impact of these differences on children.

Empirical study exploring the long-term effect of an experienced relationship with the natural world on a person's sense of meaning and purpose as well as the development of a spiritual sense of self would also be helpful in validating the findings stated in the current study. This might be done in the form of interview and questionnaire.

For those interested in validating findings such as those stated in this study with neuroscience, experiments measuring differences in brain waves or brain activity could be conducted with children taking part in nature-based programs. Findings from this kind of scientific experiment could be validated against qualitative data collected in interviews.

## Implications of the Contribution from the Transference Dialogues

The transference dialogues revealed an important aspect of the earth-human unity described in this study. The overlap and connection between abuse of the child and abuse of the natural world was clearly stated in the dialogues. Based on this and the findings from the literature, abuse of the natural world impacts the child's development of a sense of self. When adults treat the natural world as a "collection of objects" (Berry, 1999, p. 16) this is transmitted to and inherited by the child. Abuse of the natural world impacts a child's development of a sense of self in that they learn about our relationship with the natural world with the abuse as part of the picture. In this case, abuse and destruction of the natural world is normalized because it occurs in everyday living—it is not outside of the ordinary. Just as children learn in their own families about the dynamics of relationship and what it means to love and care for one another, so they learn about the dynamics of relationship with the natural world.

In addition, beyond conceptualizations about the natural world, or attitude, or unconscious beliefs about the natural world, it seems to me that on the level of the *unus mundus* and the continuity between psyche and matter, abuse directly affects the *unus mundus*, for it exists as a unity. Thus abuse of the child or abuse of the natural world on this level are one and the same thing. Of course, this is not to diminish the priority we would naturally place on abuse of children over some form of abuse of the natural world. Clearly, our hearts are highly attuned to other human beings and protection of children will continue to be more immediately compelling to us than protection of the natural world. However, in our compassion for children and in our desire and need to protect children from harm, it is clear that compassion does not stop with children but extends beyond them to other people and the natural world.

Our thoughts and emotions clearly have impact in the larger sense on the natural world. This we see in our willingness to pollute, to destroy natural habitats, in the expression of our anger and fear through the dropping of destructive bombs, and our fear and greed through practices such as mountaintop removal mining. If we did not have thoughts and emotions these things certainly would not be happening. It is therefore clear that our thoughts and emotions have direct impact on the natural world when they are made manifest in practices such as these; however, we do not actually know about a more subtle but immediate, direct impact of our thoughts and emotions on the natural world around us. Does the heron in the lake somehow sense my anger or despair while I drive by? Do plants "perceive" on some level our fear, or our complete negligence of the life they are? Clearly, animals respond to human beings and can have an emotional connection to people. Anyone who has had the good fortune to have the companionship of an animal will attest to this. This we can easily see. In fact, a striking example of the emotional connection between even wild animals and human beings is the case of the so-called elephant whisperer, Lawrence Anthony in South Africa (Anthony & Spence, 2009). Anthony rehabilitated elephants who were at risk of being killed for encroaching on human living areas. He somehow learned to emotionally connect with many of these incredible, majestic, and in this case, angry animals, communicating his good will to them and protecting them from the guns of less-interested human beings. When Anthony died, 20 elephants reputedly traveled to his home from 12 miles away, stayed for 3 days in apparent recognition of his passing, and then returned to their lives in their natural habitat. The mystery in this event is that the elephants traveled to his home the day after he died, of their own accord. The fact that they remembered how to find his home, as well as that they somehow knew of his death, have been the source of much marvel and appreciation for the bond that Anthony had with these elephants. Thus, not only domesticated animals, but wild animals as well have been known to have a sense of emotional connection with human beings. For some people, it is not so much a surprise to learn that animals and human beings are connected, but a surprise to learn that not everybody has this experience or believes it to be true. If human beings and animals can have this kind of connection with one another, what is to say that our thoughts and emotions do not have direct and immediate impact on the rest of the natural world?

Therefore, what surfaced in the transference dialogues, as well as other experiences throughout the course of this study contributed to the awareness that human beings and the earth are intimately connected, beyond the strictly ecological level of connection. The content of the transference dialogues, as promised in the imaginal approach to research, deepened the data collected in the study by revealing some of what may have been outside the conscious, egoic perspective of the researcher.

## Further Thoughts on the Implications of this Study for Clinical Psychology

During the final stages of the writing of this dissertation, I, along with the rest of the country and world, received news of the tragic shooting in Newtown, Connecticut. As a former teacher of children the same tender age as those taken in this event, it is impossible to fathom a loss of this magnitude. Along with the rest of the world, I grieve this senseless loss. It is a reminder of the critical importance of waking up to the reality of the world we live in where electronics and guns take the place of embodied, sensory-perceptual experiences in the natural world. It would be senseless for me to attribute Adam Lanza's empty act of heart-wrenching violence to anything I could name. How could I possibly know what happened *in* him or *to* him to cause such an act of hateful destruction; however, it seems a safe bet to say that Adam did not have a sense of connection, did not have a sense of belonging, a sense of meaning or purpose, a sense of gratitude or faith, and clearly not a sense of compassion. Was Adam acting as an individual, completely disconnected from the rest of society, or was Adam's act perhaps in part a symptom of a greater sense of separation and disconnection within our society? These are difficult questions that will go without answer for at least some time. However, the questions coming more directly as a result of this study have to do with whether we will continue to keep our eyes closed to the forms of abuse happening all around us.

Abuse of children includes trampling of the child's spiritual life by not listening to the child. Listening involves not just listening to words but to the presence of the child. Another way of listening to the child is being wholly present; it does not only involve listening to the words of the child. When we are present to the presence of a child, we are more likely to be equipped to treat the child with respect, to protect the child from harm, and to learn from the child. This has direct implications for how children are regarded within clinical psychology and within education. A shift in perspective, a shift in consciousness regarding self, spirituality, and the natural world in children promises to contribute both to the child's healthy development, as well as to the healing of the relationship between human beings and Earth.

## Closing Words

The completion of this study brings me full circle—back to the poem quoted in the introduction to this study, which came to me as a child:

I am you
You are me
We are all
All are we.

We cannot judge one another
for if we do,
It would be as though

I were not you
You were not me
We were not all
All were not we.

It is only now, after a lengthy research process and decades of life experience that I can fully appreciate, and attempt to live into, the simple but complete wisdom that seemed to come to me like a treasure out of the starry night sky.

In conclusion, one of the great spiritual teachers of today, Thich Nhat Hanh, shared his counsel on healing people and healing the planet in an interview with Jo Confino (2012). In Confino's article, Hanh is reported to believe that "the lack of meaning and connection in peoples' lives [is] the cause of our addiction to consumerism. . . . It is vital we recognise and respond to the stress we are putting on Earth if civilisation is to survive" (para. 2). Seeing human beings and the earth as separate is a major part of this problem, according to Hanh. He advises a new relationship with Earth in order to rectify the problems of civilization:

> You carry Mother Earth within you. She is not outside of you. Mother Earth is not just your environment. . . .
>
> Breathe in and be aware of your body and look deeply into it and realize you are the Earth and your consciousness is also the consciousness of the earth. . . . So the healing of the people should go together with the healing of the Earth. (as cited in Confino, 2012, para. 3)

# References

Adams, M. V. (2008). The archetypal school. In P. Young-Eisendrath & T. Dawson (Eds.) *The Cambridge companion to Jung* (pp. 107-124). New York, NY: Cambridge University Press.

Adams, W. W. (1999). The interpermeation of self and world: Empirical research, existential phenomenology, and transpersonal psychology. *Journal of Phenomenological Psychology, 30*(2), 39-67.

Adams, W. W. (2005). Ecopsychology and phenomenology: Toward a collaborative engagement. *Existential Analysis, 16*(2), 269-283.

Anderson, B. W. (1999). *The contours of old testament theology.* Minneapolis, MN: Augsburg Fortress.

Anthony, L. with Spence, L G. (2009). *The elephant whisperer.* New York, NY: St. Martin's Press.

Assagioli, R. (1959). Dynamic psychology and psychosynthesis. Retrieved from http://www.psykosyntese.dk/a-175/

Assagioli, R., with Vargiu, J. (1976). The superconscious and the self. Retrieved from http://www.psykosyntese.dk/a-172/

Banai, E., Mikuliner, M., & Shaver, P. R. (2005). Selfobject needs in Kohut's self psychology: Links with attachment, self-cohesion, affect regulation, and adjustment. *Psychoanalytic Psychology, 22*(2), 224–260.

Beebe, B., & Lachmann, F. M. (2003). The relational turn in psychoanalysis: A dyadic systems view from infant research. *Contemporary Psychoanalysis, 39*(3), 379-409.

Benson, P. L. (2006). The science of child and adolescent spiritual development: Definitional, theoretical, and field-building challenges. In E. C. Roehlkepartain, P. E. King, L. Wagener, & P. Benson (Eds.), *The handbook of spiritual development in childhood and adolescence* (pp. 484-498). Thousand Oaks, CA: Sage.

Benson, P. L. (2008). Foreword. In R. M. Lerner, R. W. Roesner, & E. Phelps (Eds.), *Positive youth development and spirituality: From theory to research* (pp. vii-x). West Conshohocken, PA: Templeton Foundation Press.

Benson, P. L., Roehlkepartain, E. C., & Rude, S. P. (2003). Spiritual
    Development in Childhood and Adolescence: Toward a Field of
    Inquiry. *Applied Developmental Sciences, 7*(3), 204-212.

Berry, T. (1999). *The Great Work.* New York, NY: Bell Tower.

Berry, T. (2006). *The Dream of the earth.* San Francisco, CA: Sierra
    Club Books.

Brinthaupt, T. M., & Lipka, R. P. (1992). *The self: Definitional and
    methodological issues.* Albany: State University of New York Press.

Bromberg, P. M. (1996). Standing in the spaces: The multiplicity
    of self and the psychoanalytic relationship. *Contemporary
    Psychoanalysis, 32,* 509-535.

Camic, P. M., Rhodes, J. E., & Yardley, L. (2003). Naming the
    stars: Integrating qualitative methods into psychological
    research. In P. Camic, J. Rhodes, & L. Yardley (Eds.),
    *Qualitative research in psychology: Expanding perspectives in
    methodology and design* (pp. 3-15).Washington, DC: American
    Psychological Association.

Card, C. R. (1991, Spring-Summer). The archetypal view of C. G.
    Jung and Wolfgang Pauli. *Psychological Perspectives, 24,* 23-33.

Carson, R. (1998). *The sense of wonder.* New York, NY: HarperCollins.

Cobb, E. (1977). *The ecology of imagination in childhood.* Putnam, CT:
    Spring.

Coles, R. (1990). *The spiritual life of children.* Boston, MA: Houghton.

Collin, S. (2010). *Dictionary of computing.* London, UK: A&C Black.

Colman, W. (2008). On being, knowing and having a self. *Journal of
    Analytical Psychology, 53,* 351-366.

Confino, J. (2012, February 20). Thich Nhat Hanh: Connect with and
    love mother earth to heal the planet. *Common Dreams.* Retrieved
    from http://www.commondreams
    .org/headline/2012/02/20-0

Coope, J. (2010). Ecopsychology and the historian: Some notes on
    the work of Theodore Roszak. *European Journal of Ecopsychology
    1,* 4-18.

Corbett, L. (1996). *The religious function of the psyche.* London,
    England: Routledge.

Crowder, C. (2000). Humanity. In A. Hastings, A. Mason, & H.
    Pyper (Eds.), *The Oxford companion to Christian thought.*

Cunningham, P. (2012). *Bridging psychological science and transpersonal spirit: A primer of transpersonal psychology.* Unpublished manuscript, Psychology Department, Rivier College, Nashua, NH.

De Laszlo, V. S. (1990). Introduction. In V. S. De Laszlo (Ed.), *The basic writings of C. G. Jung* (pp. xiii-xxii). Princeton, NJ: Princeton University Press.

Edinger, E. F. (1972). *Ego and archetype: Individuation and the religious function.* London, England: Shambhala.

Fonagy, P., Gergely, G., Jurist, E. L., & Target, M. (2002). *Affect regulation, mentalization, and the development of the self.* New York, NY: Other Press.

Fordham, M. (1994). *Children as individuals.* London, England: Free Association Books.

Fordham, M. (2002). *Explorations into the self.* London, England: Karnac Books.

Forsythe, J. (1997). *Faith and human transformation: A dialogue between psychology and theology.* Lanham, MD: University Press of America.

Fowler, J. W. (1981). *Stages of faith: The psychology of human development and the quest for meaning.* San Francisco, CA: HarperCollins.

Freud, S. (1967). *Moses and monotheism* (K. Jones, Trans). New York, NY: Knopf. (Original work published 1937)

Freud, S. (1989). The future of an illusion. In J. Strachey (Ed. & Trans.), *The standard edition of the complete psychological works of Sigmund Freud* (Vol. 11, pp. 59-138). New York, NY: Norton. (Original work published 1927)

Goodstein, L. (2012, September 18). A faded piece of papyrus refers to Jesus' wife. *The New York Times.* Retrieved from http://www.nytimes.com/2012/09/19/us/historian-says-piece-of-papyrus-refers-to-jesus-wife.html?ref=opinion.

Graves, R. (1960). *The Greek myths: Complete edition.* London, England: Penguin.

Hardy, A. (1983). Foreword. In E. Robinson, *The original vision: A study of the religious experience of childhood* (pp. 3-6). New York, NY: Seabury Press.

Hart, T. (2003). *The secret spiritual world of children.* Makawao, HI: Inner Ocean.

Harter, S. (1999). *The construction of the self: A developmental perspective.* New York, NY: Guilford Press.

Hay, D., & Nye, R. (2006). *The spirit of the child.* London, England: Kingsley.

Helminski, K. E. (1992). *Living presence: The Sufi way to mindfulness and the essential self.* New York, NY: Penguin.

Hergenhahn, B. R. (2005). *An introduction to the history of psychology.* Belmont, CA: Wadsworth.

Hill, P. C., & Pargament, K. I. (2003). Advances in the conceptualization and measurement of religion and spirituality: Implications for physical and mental health. *American Psychologist, 58,* 64-74.

Hogenson, G. B. (2004). Archetypes: Emergence and the psyche's deep structure. In J. Cambray & L. Carter (Eds.) *Analytical psychology: Comtemporary perspectives in Jungian analysis* (pp. 32-55). New York, NY: Brunner-Routledge.

Hood, R. W., Hill, P. C., & Spilka, B. (2009). *The psychology of religion* (4th ed.). New York, NY: Guilford Press.

Hyde, B. (2008). *Children and spirituality.* London, England: Kingsley.

International Community for Ecopsychology. (2004). Home page. Retrieved from http://www.ecopsychology.org/

Jacobson, E. (1964). *The self and the object world.* New York, NY: International Universities Press.

Jacoby, M. (1990). *Individuation and Narcissism.* London, England: Routledge.

Jacoby, M. (2008). *Jungian psychotherapy and contemporary infant research.* New York, NY: Routledge.

James, W. (1890). *The principles of psychology, volume 1.* New York, NY: Holt.

James, W. (2008). *The varieties of religious experience.* Rockville, MD: Arc Manor.

Johnson, C. N. (2008). The spirit of spiritual development. In R. E. Lerner, R. W. Roesner, & E. Phelps (Eds.). *Positive youth development and spirituality: From theory to research* (pp. 25-41). West Conshohocken, PA: Templeton Foundation Press.

Jung, C. G. (1938). *Psychology and religion.* New Haven: Yale University Press.

Jung, C. G. (1954). *The symbolic life* (Vol. 18). New York, NY: Princeton University Press.

Jung, C. G. (1969). Aion: Researched into the phenomenology of the self. In H. Read, M. Fordham, & G. Adler (Eds.), *The collected works of C. G. Jung* (R. F. C. Hull, Trans) (Vol. 9). Princeton, NJ: Princeton University Press. (Original work published 1951)

Jung, C. G. (1969). On the nature of the psyche. In H. Read, M. Fordham, & G. Adler (Eds.), *The collected works of C. G. Jung* (R. F. C. Hull, Trans) (2nd ed., Vol. 8, , pp. 159-236). Princeton, NJ: Princeton University Press. (Original work published in 1947)

Jung, C. G. (1970). On the psychology and pathology of so-called occult phenomena. In H. Read, M. Fordham, & G. Adler (Eds.), *The collected works of C. G. Jung* (R. F. C. Hull, Trans) (2nd ed., Vol. 1, pp. 3-88). Princeton, NJ: Princeton University Press. (Original work published 1902)

Jung, C. G. (1989). *Memories, dreams, reflections* (A. Jaffé, Ed.) (R. Winston & C. Winston, Trans.) (Rev. ed.). New York, NY: Vintage Books. (Original work published 1961)

Jung, C. G. (1990). The relations between the ego and the unconscious [Excerpt]. In V. S. De Laszlo (Ed.), *The basic writings of C. G. Jung* (pp. 136-229). Princeton, NJ: Princeton University Press. (Original work published 1928)

Jung, C. G. (2008). *The earth has a soul: C. G. Jung on nature, technology and modern life* (M. Sabini, Ed.). Berkeley, CA: North Atlantic Books.

Kellert, S. (2002). Experiencing nature: Affective, cognitive, and evaluative development in children. In P. H. Kahn, & S. R. Kellert (Eds.), *Children and nature: Psychological, sociocultural, and evolutionary investigations* (pp. 117-152). Cambridge: Massachusetts Institute of Technology Press.

Kellert, S. (2005). *Building for life: Designing and understanding the human-nature connection.* Washington, DC: Island Press.

Kneezel, T. T., & Emmons, R. A. (2006). Personality and spiritual development. In E. C. Roehlkepartain, P. E. King, L. Wagener, &

P. Benson (Eds.), *The handbook of spiritual development in childhood and adolescence* (pp. 266-278). Thousand Oaks, CA: Sage.

Kohler, L. (1957). *Old Testament theology.* Philadelphia, PA: Westminster.

Kohut, H., & Wolf, E. S. (1978). The disorders of the self and their treatment. *International Journal of Psycho-Analysis, 59,* 413-426. Retrieved from PEP Archive database. (Accession No: IJP.059.0413A)

Küng, H. (1990). *Freud and the problem of God* (E. Quinn, Trans.). New Haven, CT: Yale University Press. (Original work published 1978)

Lachmann, F. M. (2004). Identity and self: Historical antecedents and developmental precursors. *International Forum of Psychoanalysis, 13*(4), 246-254. Retrieved from PEP Archive database. (Accession No. IFP.013.0246A)

Lachmann, F.M. (2011). *Transforming narcissism: Reflections on empathy, humor, and expectations.* New York, NY: Analytic Press.

Lachmann, F.M., & Beebe, B. (1989). Oneness fantasies revisited. *Psychoanalytic Psychology, 6*(2), 137-149.

Lerner, R. M., Lamb, M. E., & Freund, A. (Eds.). (2010). *The handbook of life-span development: Vol. 2.* Hoboken, NJ: Wiley.

Lerner, R. M., Roesner, R. W., & Phelps, E. (Eds.). (2008). *Positive youth development and spirituality: From theory to research.* West Conshohocken, PA: Templeton Foundation Press.

Lichtenberg, J. D. (1989). *Psychoanalysis and motivation.* Hillsdale, NJ: Analytic Press.

Lichtenberg, J. D. (2001). *Self and motivational systems: Toward a theory of psychoanalytic technique.* New York, NY: Routledge.

Lichtenberg, J. D., Lachmann, F. M., & Fossage, J. L. (2011). *Psychoanalysis and motivational systems: A new look.* New York, NY: Routledge.

Louv, R. (2005). *Last child in the woods: Saving our children from nature-deficit-disorder.* Chapel Hill, NC: Algonquin.

Macy, J. (2007). *World as lover world as self: Courage for global justice and ecological renewal.* Berkeley, CA: Parallax Press.

Main, S. (2008). *Childhood re-imagined: Images and narratives of development in analytical psychology.* New York, NY: Routledge.

Maslow, A. (1969a). The farther reaches of human nature. *Journal of Transpersonal Psychology, 1*(1), 1-9.

Maslow, A. (1969b). The various meanings of transcendence. *Journal of Transpersonal Psychology, 1*(1), 56-66.

Maslow, A. (1971). *The farther reaches of human nature.* New York, NY: Viking Press.

Maslow, A. (1987). *Motivation and personality.* New York, NY: Harper.

Maslow, A. (1999). *Toward a psychology of being.* New York, NY: Wiley.

McAdams, D. (1993). *The stories we live by: Personal myths and the making of the self.* New York, NY: Guilford Press.

McAdams, D. P., & Cox, K. S. (2010). Self and identity across the life span. In M. Lamb, A. Freund, & M. Lerner (Eds.), *The handbook of lifespan development, volume 2: Social and emotional development* (pp. 158-207). Hoboken, NJ: Wiley.

Miller, S. (1972). The will, interview with Roberto Assagioli by Stuart Miller. Retrieved from http://www.psykosyntese.dk/a-196/

Mitchell, S. A. (1991). Contemporary perspectives on self: Toward an integration. *Psychoanalytic Dialogues, 1*, 121-148. Retrieved from PEP Archive database. (Accession No. PD.001.0121A)

Montessori, M. (1966). *The secret of childhood* (M. J. Costelloe). New York, NY: Ballantine Books. (Original work published 1936)

Montessori, M. (1948). *The discovery of the child* (M. J. Costelloe). Oxford, UK: Clio Press.

Montessori, M. (1988). *The absorbent mind* (C. A. Claremont, Trans.). Oxford, UK: Clio Press.

Montessori, M. (1989). *To educate the human potential.* Oxford, UK: Clio Press.

Myers, B. K. (1997). *Young children and spirituality.* New York, NY: Routledge.

Neumann, E. (1995). *The origins and history of consciousness* (R. F. C. Hull, Trans.). Princeton, NJ: Princeton University Press. (Original work published 1954)

Newberg, A., & Newberg, S. K. (2006). A neuropsychological perspective on spiritual development. In E. C. Roehlkepartain, P. E. King, L. Wagener, & P. Benson (Eds.), *The handbook of spiritual development in childhood and adolescence* (pp. 183-196). Thousand Oaks, CA: Sage.

Nidich, S., Nidich, R. & Alexander, C. (2000) . Moral development and higher states of consciousness. *Journal of Adult Development, 7*(4), 217-225.

Norfleet, N. (2010, June 11). Rare photo found of slave children. *The News & Observer.* (p. 3B).

Palmer, R. L. (1969). *Hermeneutics.* Evanston, IL: Northwestern University Press.

Parker, S. (2006). Measuring faith development. *Journal of Psychology and Theology, 34*(4), 337-348.

Ratcliff, D., & Nye, R. (2006). Childhood spirituality: Strengthening the research foundation. In E. C. Roehlkepartain, P. E. King, L. Wagener, & P. Benson (Eds.), *The handbook of spiritual development in childhood and adolescence* (pp. 473-483). Thousand Oaks, CA: Sage.

Robinson, E. (1983). *The original vision: A study of the religious experience of childhood.* New York, NY: Seabury Press.

Roehlkepartain, E. G., Benson, P. L., Scales, P. C., Kimball, L., & King, P. E. (2008). *With their own voices: A global exploration of how today's young people experience and think about spiritual development.* Minneapolis, MN: Search Institute, Center for Spiritual Development in Childhood and Adolescence.

Roehlkepartain, E. C., King, P. E., Wagener, L., & Benson, P. (Eds.). (2006a). *The handbook of spiritual development in childhood and adolescence.* Thousand Oaks, CA: Sage.

Roehlkepartain, E. C., King, P. E., Wagener, L., & Benson, P. (2006b). Preface. In *The handbook of spiritual development in childhood and adolescence* (xiii-xiv). Thousand Oaks, CA: Sage.

Roehlkepartain, E. C., Benson, P. L., King, P. E., & Wagener, L. M. (2006). Spiritual development in childhood and adolescence: Moving into the mainstream. In E. C. Roehlkepartain, P. E. King, L. Wagener, & P. Benson (Eds.), *The handbook of spiritual development in childhood and adolescence* (pp. 1-15). Thousand Oaks, CA: Sage.

Romanyshyn, R. (2007). *The wounded researcher: Research with soul in mind.* New Orleans, LA: Spring Journal.

Roszak, T. (1995). Where psyche meets Gaia. In T. Roszak, M. E. Gomes, & A. D. Kanner (Eds.), *Ecopsychology: Restoring the earth, healing the mind*. San Francisco, CA: Sierra Club Books.

Roszak, T. (1998, September). Ecopsychology: Eight principles. *Ecopsychology on-line*. Retrieved from http://ecopsychology. athabascau.ca/Final/intro.htm

Roszak, T. (2001). *The voice of the earth: An exploration of ecopsychology*. Grand Rapids, MI: Phanes Press.

S0phia Inkpen. (2012, January 17). Venice@Prada [Web log post]. Retrieved November 20, 2012 from http://virtualtraveling. blogspot.com/2012/01/venice-prada.html

Samuels, A. (1998). Will the post-Jungians survive? In A. Casement (Ed.), *Post-Jungians today: Key papers in contemporary analytical psychology* (pp. 15-32). London, UK: Routledge.

Scarlett, W. G., & Warren, A. E. A. (2010). Religious and spiritual development across the life span: A behavioral and social science perspective. In M. Lamb, A. Freund, & M. Lerner (Eds.), *The handbook of lifespan development, volume 2: Social and emotional development* (pp. 631-682). Hoboken, NJ: Wiley.

Schroll, M. A. (2007). Wrestling with Arne Naess: A chronicle of ecopsychology's origins. *The Trumpeter, 23*(1), 28-57.

Search Institute (2008). Engaging international advisors in creating a shared understanding of spiritual development. Retrieved from http://archive-org.com /page/1124696/2013-01-12/http://www.search-institute.org/ csd/major-projects /definition-update

Shore, A. (1994). *Affect regulation and the origin of the self.* Hillsdale, NJ: Erlbaum.

Sidoli, M. (1998). Archetypal patterns, mental representations, and replicative processes in infancy. In A. Casement (Ed.), *Post-Jungians today: Key papers in contemporary analytical psychology* (pp. 103-115). London, England: Routledge.

Siegel, A. M. (1996). *Heinz Kohut and the psychology of the self.* London, UK: Routledge.

Simms, E. (2008). *The child in the world: Embodiment, time, and language in early childhood.* Detroit, MI: Wayne State University Press.

Soloman, H. M. (2008). The developmental school. In P. Young-Eisendrath & T. Dawson (Eds.), *The Cambridge companion to Jung* (pp. 125-146). New York, NY: Cambridge University Press.

Sorensen, K., & Birkholm, L. (n.d.). Roberto Assagioli: His life and work. Retrieved from http://www.psykosyntese.dk/a-146/

Sroufe, A., Egeland, B., Carlson, E. A., & Collins, W. A. (2005). *The development of the person.* New York, NY: Guilford Press.

Stein, M. (1998). *Jung's map of the soul: An introduction.* La Salle, IL: Carus.

Steiner, R. (1974). *Inner aspect of the social question* (C. Davy, Trans.). London, England: Steiner Press. (Original work published 1968)

Steiner, R. (1997). *The roots of education* (Trans. unknown). New York, NY: Anthroposophic Press. (Original work published 1968)

Stern, D. (1985). *The interpersonal world of the infant.* New York, NY: Basic Books.

Stolorow, R. D. (1997). Dynamic, dyadic, intersubjective systems: An evolving paradigm for psychoanalysis. *Psychoanalytic Psychology,* *14*(3), 337-346.

Stolorow, R. D., & Atwood, G. E. (1992). *Contexts of being: The intersubjective foundations of psychological life.* Hillsdale, NJ: Analytic Press.

Stolorow, R. D., & Atwood, G. E. (1994). The myth of the isolated mind. *Progress in Self Psychology, 10,* 233-251. Retrieved from PEP Archive database. (Accession No. PSP.010.0233A)

Thelen, E., & Smith, L. B. (1994). *A dynamic systems approach to the development of cognition and action.* Cambridge, MA: Bradford Books/MIT Press.

Toben, C. (2012). *Recovering a sense of the sacred: Conversations with Thomas Berry.* Whitsett, NC: Timberlake Earth Sanctuary Press.

Vickers, B. (1986). *Occult scientific mentalities.* Cambridge, UK: Cambridge University Press.

von Franz, M-L. (1980). *Alchemy: An introduction to the symbolism and the psychology.* Toronto, Canada: Inner City Books.

Walker, L. J., & Reimer, K. S. (2006). The relationship between moral and spiritual development. In E. C. Roehlkepartain, P.E. King, L. Wagener, & P. Benson (Eds.), *The handbook of spiritual development in childhood and adolescence* (pp. 224-238). Thousand Oaks, CA: Sage.

Wilson, E. O. (1984). *Biophilia.* Cambridge, MA: Harvard University Press.

Winnicott, D. W. (1987). *The maturational processes and the facilitating environment.* London, England: Hogarth Press.

Wolf, E. S. (1988). *Treating the self: Elements of clinical self psychology.* New York, NY: Guilford Press.

*Appendix One*

# Transcript of the Transference Dialogue

In accord with the alchemical hermeneutic approach of waiting with hospitality, I decided to write in a small journal that I adopted for this process and for dialoguing with myself about my research. I just wrote about the process up to this point as a way of keeping myself as loose as possible and not neurotically waiting for the voice of god to begin speaking to me. I became sensorially hyper-aware. I felt very tired and very aware of the pain and fatigue in my neck that hadn't just started but was very persistent. In the journal I wrote,

nervous

Who does the work serve?

*The plants, trees, animals, all of creation. For when there is abuse, all are wounded.*

When I look back at this now, I can't remember if that is something I've read, or where it came from. I'm tired, sleepy, want to go to sleep. My neck aches and is so tired. My body seems to be speaking to me, through pain and fatigue. Why does my neck hurt? Who is the pain in my neck? I am a child again, I am a pain in my father's neck. I am too much work, too much to take care of. I am troublesome. In the wait, although I tell myself I should be in an altered state—a subdued state, a dream state, I feel I must be very careful not to do anything wrong. Rather than letting go, I'm almost more conscious . . . self-conscious.

The writing continues:

> When I asked the questions aloud, and then began taking
> pictures of the research altar, Meliah began to want my atten-
> tion. She stood up and put her front paws on my leg—pick me
> up, pick me up. She became nervous, needy, and she seemed
> very concerned about what I was taking pictures of. When I
> picked her up and put her in my lap she was shaking a bit,
> seemed nervous. I wonder if she picked up on some energies—
> beings that responded to these questions about the work.
>
> My neck hurts. It tires me.

I did not consider this journaling to be a response from the "others" as
I wrote. I thought of it as my own musings and I felt confident that at
some point the "others" would in fact speak to me. The writing continues:

> It's raining today. It's been raining all day. I think it started
> raining yesterday. When I asked the question about whom the
> works serves on an archetypal level, I recalled how in my last
> paper for Dr. Romanyshyn I had written that I didn't want to
> ask the questions at that point because I wasn't fully prepared;
> that I didn't want to do the rain dance before I had a rain barrel
> at the ready. (I hear geese laughing outside.) So when I asked
> the question today and heard the rain on the skylight above me,
> it made me think: perhaps on some level I had indeed already
> asked the question and the rain was coming down. Could there
> be some tension, some anger from nature directed toward me?
> I began to wonder this because when I was writing the above
> and just got to the point of the rain dance, it seemed like I heard
> geese laughing at this thought, as if I can have anything to do
> with whether it rains or not. Or perhaps the anger is expressed
> in there being so much rain right now that I could become
> overwhelmed. There goes a big gust of wet wind outside. I can
> hear the wind chimes in their buffeted song. Maybe nature's
> first response to being tapped into is anger. Meliah just shivered
> on my lap. Is she cold, or what? Maybe nature would have us

know that it is none too happy with "nice" people who have good intentions and meanwhile the earth gets ravaged and abused. I just noticed hunger pangs in my stomach. Sleepy, achy. Was it wrong to take the pictures when I did, in the middle of preparing a sacred altar to the work?

I stopped writing at that point and closed the journal. I was finished for the day. The wait would continue and again, I had confidence that the "others" would make themselves heard when it was time.

It was either that night or a night or two later that I had a dream:

> Walking the dogs. Jasper. Behind a small ridge next to road, a fox going after a cat? At first, I was curious. I see it's a fox and I'm kind of excited because foxes are hard to see. I just walk along and don't do anything. I'm a little concerned because I don't want the fox to hurt the cat, or my dog. Then a woman comes out of her house, seeing the fox. She makes me realize the fox is dangerous and should not be indulged. I think it will be easy to scare him off. I am sort of identifying with it. Then I start to get nervous because it's walking along with me and Jasper. I realize I need to scare it away but then we start to make eye contact and I realize I might be sending it a challenging message. I try not to have eye contact. I keep trying not to have eye contact but to scare him off. His eyes begin to get fierce and I begin to get very nervous. I'm afraid for my dog and then myself. I wake up. I try to rehearse dream so I won't forget. It's the middle of the night and I don't want to get up. Something compels me to write it down. I search for pad and pen. Eventually, I must get up and write it.

The next time I sit down to work on my concept paper, I just start writing questions. I am trying to come up with interview questions for children and I am playing with different ways of phrasing my research question. I write:

> How does a sense of connection with the natural world contribute to the spiritual development of children?

Then, my handwriting seems to have changed as I look back at what I wrote next. It seems very odd, disturbing:

> *dead people, dead children—children who have been hacked up brutally, children who have been abused, neglected, brutalized. children who have been given away.*

> *The work is for the child. The abuse, neglected child, the aborted child, the abandoned child, the murdered child. The work gives voice to these children, who did not get to speak when they were living. The child who was not protected, not nurtured, not cared for in the way the child expects to be cared for. The child in me. The child in each of my siblings. The child in each of my parents—the sexually abused child, the physically and emotionally abused child. The child of an alcoholic, the child of immigrants, the uneducated child, the child bride, the child married off to a stranger. The child wants to speak.*

What does the child want to say?

> *The abandoned, neglected, abused child.*

> *There are so many things I would have told you if given the chance. My life was cut short either through death, abuse or neglect. I had precious gifts to share, wisdom to impart, joy. But these were lost in the treacheries done upon me. The foundation of my being was swept away, there is carnage in its place. I stand upon an edifice of bones. The flower that I was to become withered and died while still in bud. I want you to unfold me. Love me into existence—love the stillborn blossom within the shriveled bud into existence to hear what I meant to way. It won't be easy. The writing will unfold petal upon petal but I am like a peoni with many, many tightly packed petals, not like a tulip with clean, well-defined petals. The writing will bring each petal forth to flower.*

> *The tired child, the burdened child, the anxious child, the weary child, the confused child, the bewildered child, the fretting child. So many children waiting to be heard. A child wants to be heard. A*

*child "speaks" herself into being but only becomes when she is heard. You ask if a tree falls in the woods....you could easily ask, if a child speaks in the wilderness does anybody hear? Does the child exist? When you listen to a child, you give the child a chance to come into being. When you don't listen, her words fall upon the forest floor and lie fallow in hopes of being given another opportunity.*

*A child needs validation of being heard to come into being.*

*So many children have not come fully into being because they haven't been heard.*
*But when there is neglect, abuse, trampling under foot, there is great damage to the child. The child is hurt, the child is wounded, the child, like nature, needs care, needs to be heard, needs to be treasured.*

*The child is not an innocent. The child has wisdom and also brings darkness. But when children bring darkness, that too wants to be heard. You think of the child as less than adult, not fully human. No, the child is just in a different state of development and a source of great wisdom to adults if they can listen without belittling.*

*The child has a natural affinity for nature and considers its first mother to be nature.*

*Write about the child.*

Fell asleep head on arms on desk.
The voice of the child continues to speak but I couldn't bring it out of sleep.

*Appendix Two*

## Article and Photograph from
### *The News & Observer*

The photo was found at a moving sale in Charlotte, accompanied by a document detailing the sale of John, left, for $1,150 in 1854. An album including the photo sold for $30,000 to a New York collector.

# Rare photo found of slave children

## Portrait was discovered in an N.C. attic

**By Nicole Norfleet**
THE ASSOCIATED PRESS

RALEIGH – A haunting 150-year-old photo found in a North Carolina attic shows a young black child named John, barefoot and wearing ragged clothes, perched on a barrel next to an unidentified young boy.

Art historians think it's an extremely rare Civil War-era photograph of children who were either slaves at the time or recently emancipated.

The photo, which may have been taken in the early 1860s, was a testament to a dark part of American history, said Will Stapp, a photographic historian and founding curator of the National Portrait Gallery's photographs department at the Smithsonian Institution.

"It's a very difficult and poignant piece of American history," he said. "What you are looking at when you look at this photo are two boys who were victims of that history."

In April, the photo was found at a moving sale in Charlotte, accompanied by a document detailing the sale of John for $1,150, not a small sum in 1854.

New York collector Keya Morgan said he paid $30,000 for the photo album including the photo of the young boys and several family pictures, and $20,000 for the sale document. Morgan said the deceased owner of the home where the photo was found was thought to be a descendant of John.

A portrait of slave children is rare, Morgan said.

"I buy stuff all the time, but this shocked me," he said.

What makes the picture an even more compelling find is that several art experts said it was created by the photography studio of Mathew Brady, a famous 19th-century photographer known for his portraits of historical figures such as President Abraham Lincoln and Confederate Gen. Robert E. Lee.

Stapp said the photo was probably not taken by Brady but by Timothy O'Sullivan, one of Brady's apprentices.

In 1862, O'Sullivan famously photographed a group of some of the first slaves liberated after Lincoln issued his preliminary Emancipation Proclamation.

Such photos were circulated in the North by abolitionists to garner support for the Union during the Civil War, said Harold Holzer, an author of several books about Lincoln. Holzer works as an administrator at the Metropolitan Museum of Art.

Most of the photos depicted adult slaves who had been beaten or whipped, he said.

The photo of the two boys is more subtle, Holzer said, which may be why it wasn't widely circulated and remained unpublished for so long.

"To me, it's such a moving and astonishing picture," he said.

For now, Morgan said, he is keeping the photo in his personal collection, but he said he has had an inquiry to sell the photo to the Metropolitan Museum of Art.

He said he is considering participating in the creation of a video-documentary about John.

"This kid was abused and mistreated, and people forgot about him," Morgan said. "He doesn't even exist in history. And to know that there were a million children who were like him, I've never seen another photo like that that speaks so much for children."

A document detailing the sale of a slave named John provides some insight into the horrors of the slave trade, collector Keya Morgan says.

Made in the USA
Middletown, DE
17 February 2018